The Which? Guide to
Starting Your Own Business

As this book went to press, the government launched its Millennium Bug Campaign to help businesses of all sizes beat the problem that many date-dependent devices, which recognise only the final two digits of a year – most obviously computers, but all sorts of other business equipment too – will fail to cope with the change from the year '99 to '00.

The Millennium Bug Campaign is run by Action 2000, sponsored by the Department of Trade and Industry. Among other goals, it exists to provide direct support for small and medium businesses, with, for instance:

○ a national hotline on (0845) 601 2000
○ a guidebook and help sheets
○ a web site on http://www.open.gov.uk/bug2000.htm

Whatever the size of your business, act sooner rather than later.

The Which? Guide to Starting Your Own Business

CONSUMERS' ASSOCIATION

Which? Books are commissioned and researched by
Consumers' Association and published by
Which? Ltd, 2 Marylebone Road, London NW1 4DF
Email address: books@which.net

Distributed by The Penguin Group:
Penguin Books Ltd, 27 Wrights Lane, London W8 5TZ

First edition (as *Starting Your Own Business*) 1983
Second edition 1992
Revised editions 1984, 1985, 1986, 1988, 1993, 1994
Third edition (as *The Which? Guide to Starting Your Own Business*)
June 1996
Fourth edition March 1998

British Library Cataloguing in Publication Data
A catalogue record for this book is available from the British Library

ISBN 0 85202 709 5

For a full list of *Which?* books, please write to Which? Books, Castlemead,
Gascoyne Way, Hertford X, SG14 1LH, or access our web site at http://www.which.net

Editorial revisions by Jane Vass with help from Philippa Marfleet; revisions to Chapter 10 by
Richard Wentk

Cover and text design by Kyzen Creative Consultants

Typeset by Saxon Graphics Ltd, Derby
Printed and bound in Great Britain by Clays Ltd, Bungay, Suffolk

Contents

★ An asterisk next to the name of an organisation in the text indicates that the address can be found in this section

Introduction

The world of work has changed dramatically over the past 20 years. While there have always been entrepreneurs who would never have settled into full-time employment, the end of the 'job for life' culture means that these days many more people at some time or another consider 'going it alone'. The rewards in terms of personal fulfilment can be considerable: a chance to develop a business idea or skill of your own, an opportunity to combine work more easily with your lifestyle, or a move into consultancy for a varied and interesting range of clients.

On the other hand, self-employment can come to control you – body, mind and spirit. According to Dun and Bradstreet, the business information company, 50 per cent of businesses cease trading in the first four years. Even some of the 50 per cent who are still in business after that time probably didn't realise at first just what they were letting themselves in for. To give yourself the best chance of success you need advice and information – not just on the formalities and practicalities but also on the potential pitfalls and difficulties.

If you are changing from being employed to becoming self-employed, and perhaps, sooner or later, employing others, you will inevitably have to make adjustments to your values and priorities. You will need to be highly motivated, for no one else will push you to achieve your goals; you will also need enthusiasm, commitment and drive. A flexible approach will help ensure that you can survive and thrive whatever the political and economic conditions. You may also need support from your family because working for yourself is not the same as having a nine-to-five job. Finally, you need to be realistic about what you can achieve and be prepared for hard work.

A key to success is careful preparation and thought. You will need to investigate your potential market, and how to reach it: do you intend to provide a product or service that the public actually wants? You may need to raise start-up finance, find premises, comply with official requirements, get to grips with accounts and the tax system, chase your debtors and protect your investment from those who seek a free ride on the back of your ideas.

In covering all these topics, and more, this book tries to give you an insight into the many things you need to be aware of, when starting your own business, and where to go for further information and advice. There has never been so much help and encouragement available to small businesses, from both official bodies and other organisations, so use it. You are likely to have a lot to learn and it is important that you can do so as efficiently as possible so that you can concentrate on the central issue – building your business.

Chapter 1

Having what it takes

To run your own business, of whatever kind, you need not only some capital and some capability but also a certain flair, toughness and some good fortune. Very few of the people who start a small business have enough of both flair and luck to end up as millionaires. You might be one of them; more probably you will succeed in making a living, while enjoying the satisfaction of independence and of doing work you have chosen for yourself.

To achieve this, you must be committed; you must choose a business project that is right for you; and you must prepare yourself as thoroughly as possible before taking the plunge.

Commitment

It is no use being half-hearted when starting up a business: you should be motivated positively, not just negatively by a dislike of the job you are in, or unemployment. Your incentive should be to a large extent financial, and do not set your sights too low: from the start, your aim should be to make a reasonable living.

In becoming your own boss you may find yourself working for a harder taskmaster than any you have had previously, one who offers unlimited working hours, uncertain holidays and perhaps, to start with, less money than you were earning before. You will be exchanging the support and companionship of fellow workers for a kind of isolation in which you stand or fall by your own decisions.

There will be few executive perks, or none; you will look at these with a different eye when they have to be paid for out of your profits.

The members of your family should feel equally committed. Their moral support, quite apart from any work-support, will be

invaluable, especially during periods of difficulty and discourage-
ment. They ought to be aware that their security depends on your
success, that you may have less time for family life, and that the
rewards may be some time in coming.

Choosing your project

Anyone wanting to start a business has either found a product to
manufacture or an idea for one, or has decided to go into distribution, or to provide a service. It is no good saying to yourself, 'I want
to go into business but I don't know whether to be a manufacturer
or a distributor or to provide a service.'

Your choice of business project is a decision you alone can make,
because you are in the best position to know what your marketable
skills and capabilities are, and which of them you want to be the
foundation of your new career.

You may want to capitalise on the knowledge of a trade, the business training or the managerial experience acquired in your previous work. But if it is work that you are or were unhappy in, you may
want to strike out in a new direction.

A hobby which has made you an expert at some trade – for
instance, cabinet-making, cooking, dressmaking – can be the start
of a business, especially if you have already begun to make money
from it in your spare time: you will then have the beginnings of a
client list, and some idea of a potential market. When you approach
a bank or other organisation for a loan, you will inspire more confidence if you already have some history of successful trading. But
remember that it is a big jump from moonlighting to making a living from it, and selling a hobby-item to a few friends and relatives
may not be a good indication of its appeal to the general public or of
its economic viability.

You may have an original business idea. Perhaps you have
designed a new product that fills a gap in the market which everyone else has failed to notice; or you may have an idea for a service
which would facilitate the workings of some industry.

You may want to enter an established trade by operating a franchise or buying into a partnership, or by taking over a going concern. But if the trade is new to you, be wary; you are unlikely to be
able to master it at the same time as learning the complexities of

running a business. Bear in mind that you will be competing with people who are already established experts in the field. It is better to get your training and experience first, by working in the trade for a period, and attending any relevant training courses.

Getting off to a flying start

Most businesses have small beginnings which only involve the proprietor in the purchase of premises and equipment. But there are several ways in which the prospective businessperson (and the established businessperson wishing to expand) can take over an existing business or make use of someone else's business idea. This will, in general, involve you in a greater capital outlay, but the right decision can bring with it the knowledge that you have a good chance of making a success of the business. The other side of the coin is that you may risk financial overcommitment or taking on a business which you do not understand adequately.

In making your choice of project (assuming you have a choice), you should define your field of operations as specifically as possible, and be clear about your ultimate aims. If your ambition is to start up a business in one area and then expand elsewhere, or even to build up a great organisation, you must be sure to choose a business that is capable of such growth. If, however, your sole ambition is to make a comfortable living and sell or close down the firm when you retire, do not choose a business which can only survive by continually growing and expanding.

Some ways into your own business

If you have developed an original business idea but do not want to deal with the whole of the business side yourself, you may make an agreement with a manufacturer to make your product, retaining for yourself any part of the operation to which you can offer a unique contribution, such as design or marketing. Do not forget that you should, if possible, protect any truly novel idea (for instance, by applying for a patent), before disclosing it to any interested party.

Look around to see if you can find any other small firms, old or new, working in the same or a related field, who might be willing to pool resources with you in a network. For example, a successful merger of this kind has been achieved by a car hire firm, florist, hairdresser, photographer, video producer and dress designer, who set up a joint venture wedding services company: as well as sharing expenses, they were able to develop a common advertising and marketing policy, while remaining autonomous.

To set up such an arrangement you will have to do some research to find other firms in your line of trade in your locality. Consult your local Business Link★ (see opposite); if there is a Small Business Club in your area, it may be willing to advertise your needs among its members. There is also a network of agencies which provides a national business introduction service, known as LINC★ (Local Investment Networking Company Ltd); see Chapter 2.

Preparation

The decision of when to start will need to be related to the amount of money at your disposal: there is likely to be a period during which you will be paying all the outgoings, with little or no money coming in, while your own living expenses will still have to be met.

Begin by taking stock of your resources and assets, both human and financial. Human assets include your own skills and energy, and those of any member of your family who will be working with you.

Most people starting in business lack one or more of the basic skills needed for success. It is usually cheaper in the long run to buy in a missing skill, say a clerk or bookkeeper, than attempt all the paperwork yourself unless you really know what you are doing. Not only will you take longer than a skilled person and make more mistakes, but spending the same amount of time in using your own skill (selling, for example) will make more money for the business eventually.

Skills to learn

Certain skills, however, are worth learning, such as elementary accountancy, using a computer and administration. If you intend to have a partner, perhaps your own husband or wife, divide up between you who will learn what, at evening classes perhaps, through books or by correspondence course – quite apart from reading around the main subject of your enterprise.

Get used to the idea that, however knowledgeable you may become in your own field, there is still a lot to learn. Make sure that you take advantage of the various sources of help: a large number of

'Start your own business' training courses are available. Ask at your local reference library for the nearest 'Training Access Point', which gives information about local and national training opportunities.

You may find local evening classes that teach basic business skills, or, if you want more advanced training, you can take Open University courses, or short courses at local university or other college business schools.

Official support

You are likely to find that the problem is not too little information, but making the most of what is already there. Government support for small business is now largely decentralised and channelled through local agencies such as Training and Enterprise Councils (TECs) – Local Enterprise Councils (LECs) in Scotland.

Each TEC is an independent company, operating under a performance contract with the Government. Their boards of directors are made up primarily of chief executives or managing directors from local businesses, with the remainder being drawn from leaders of education, trade unions, voluntary organisations and the public sector.

The TEC's role is to mobilise business and other interests to establish a strategic approach to raising the levels of education and training ensuring that the necessary skills exist to support a successful economy. TECs also engender enterprising attitudes to support the start-up and development of new businesses.

You can get access to the help available from TECs and other agencies through your local Business Link★ centre (Business Connect★ in Wales, Business Shop★ in Scotland). Each centre is a partnership between Chambers of Commerce, Training and Enterprise Councils, local authorities, enterprise agencies, and other bodies, such as universities. In Northern Ireland contact the Local Enterprise Development Unit (LEDU)★ for the number of its nearest regional office. Other local agencies will be listed in the *Yellow Pages* under 'Business Enterprise Agencies' (see also Chapter 2).

Business Links (or the alternatives outside England) support new and existing small businesses by providing counselling, information, advice and business skills training. Experienced business counsellors offer independent and confidential advice over a wide range of business-related matters from preparing a business plan to finding premises, from franchising to exporting and from patents to sources of finance. Business Links may also have office equipment such as computers and photocopiers which you can use free or at a nominal charge. Where Business Links do not themselves offer a particular service, they can often refer you to an agency which does – for example, to a regional video conferencing centre.

The DTI Small Firms Division publishes a variety of free leaflets and booklets, which are available from DTI Small Firms Publications* or from Business Links. One of these leaflets is called *A Guide to Help for Small Firms*. It provides lots of useful information including sources of help and advice on finance, exporting, innovation and starting a business. If you have access to the Internet, a wealth of government information is now available at http://www.open.gov.uk

Getting advice

Anyone who has previously always been an employee may find that making decisions without any help is very difficult.

Do not be too proud to ask for advice, preferably from those qualified to give it. Ask for an appointment with a business adviser at your local Business Link. You may have friends who are professional people – accountants, bank managers, solicitors – willing to advise you, perhaps initially without charging. Or a friend who is already successfully running his or her own business may be willing to give you the benefit of experience – provided you are not going to be in competition.

Although the bank manager is employed to look after the bank's interest, which may not be the same as your interest, it can be helpful to get his or her opinion, even if the bank is not providing the funds.

It may take months before you can start. You may need to find premises, with all the delays that this involves (including, perhaps, getting planning permission). If your business project is not based on something you are doing already, it is a good idea to make it into a spare-time pursuit while continuing with your job, and thereby getting some valuable experience of the work.

About finance before you start

Whatever your project, you should have a picture in your mind of what stage you intend to have reached in one year's or two years' time, even if you cannot make anything but a very approximate forecast about this. What matters is having a forward plan, against which you will be able to monitor your progress. If things go according to plan, it will give your confidence a boost. And if things are not going as planned, you will be able to take whatever action is necessary.

There are some essential basic concepts you must understand, such as overheads, materials and labour costs, unit costs, start-up capital, working capital, short-term and medium-term finance, cash flow and a profit and loss account.

The cost of producing anything is made up of a number of elements; how many are involved depends on whether it is a product or service. Reduced to their simplest terms, they are as follows:

Cost of materials

These are materials from which products are made. The cost of materials in one year, divided by the number of units of the product manufactured in that year, gives the materials cost per unit.

For a retailer or wholesaler, the materials are the stock of goods. An agent or consultant has no materials costs.

Overheads

Generally speaking, these are the standing costs of the business which must be paid whether or not you succeed in making and selling anything.

In the annual accounts, overheads are classified under the following headings:

Salaries and wages	before-tax remuneration paid to office and sales staff, also directors' salaries and any other money drawn out of the business
Rent and rates	
Heating, lighting and other services	gas, electricity, oil, propane gas, water and sewerage, etc

Advertising/marketing	(excluding the cost of any special launch)
Printing, postage and stationery, telephone, fax	all office supplies and expenses
Motor and travel expenses	tax, insurance, servicing and repairs, petrol; expenses of travel by other means
Leasing and/or hire charges	
Insurances	
Professional fees	accountant, solicitor, patent agent
Depreciation	including motor vehicles
Interest on loans and overdraft	rough estimate
Sundry expenses	

Every single one of the overheads costs must be allowed for when you are working out what to charge for a unit of your product or an hour of your time. If you underestimate your overheads, you may find that far from making a profit, you are actually working at a loss.

Direct labour costs

In a manufacturing business, these are the before-tax wages paid to the people who actually make the product (not the wages of ancillary workers such as sales and office staff).

To find the labour cost per unit, divide the total annual labour costs by the number of product units.

In practice, labour costs should be considered as overheads, since they are fixed: you cannot as a rule hire workers when you have orders for your product, and lay them off when you have none.

Costing your products

Estimate, pessimistically, how many units of your product you will make and sell in your first year of full production, given your present resources. Work out the total overheads cost for this period. By dividing the second figure by the first, you get the overheads cost per unit. Thus, if the estimated production is 10,000 units and total overheads are £20,000, you must add £2 to the materials and labour cost of each unit, to break even.

But, of course, you want to do better than just cover your costs, so you add to your break-even figure an amount which will be your profit.

Costing in a service industry

The principle is similar, except that instead of charging per unit of product, you will charge per hour of the time spent by a member of your staff in actually doing a job. Overheads usually represent the chief element of costs of the business. If you are, for instance, a washing-machine engineer, or a plumber, your charge for an hour of time should include travelling time and expenses, the cost of tools and equipment, and the wages of the person who answers the telephone and makes out the invoices: all these are overheads. And the chief element in the overheads will be salaries or wages which have to be paid whether or not anyone is actually out on a job. To all this you must add your profit charge. When you do a job yourself, you should also charge for your time, and include a profit element.

If your total overheads costs come to £12,000 for an estimated total of 1,000 job-hours per year, your break-even price per hour will be £12. If you have to replace the washing-machine's drum or motor, you will have to charge the customer separately for materials.

What is start-up capital?

This is the 'once-and-for-all' expenditure needed to start a new business, the cash you must lay out before you have manufactured a single item, or dealt with a single client. Unless you start off in your garage with a second-hand computer, you will have to pay for some, though not necessarily all, of the following:

- premises: buying or rebuilding, conversion or even building from scratch
- plant and equipment, tools
- goodwill, if taking over an existing business
- office equipment and furniture
- installation of electricity, gas, telephone and any other services
- initial administrative costs: legal and other professional fees
- stationery: the paper, envelopes, postcards, invoices, etc. printed with the firm's name
- publicity: cost of the initial launch

- insurance: for equipment, premises, liability (public and employers', for example).

You should assess this expenditure as accurately as possible and consider ways of reducing it if necessary (for instance, by delaying the buying of any pieces of plant not immediately needed, or by leasing or hiring plant instead of buying).

When you begin to work out how much money you are going to need for your project, you must be sure to include not only the start-up capital (the money needed to get your business going) but also the working capital (the money you need to keep you going during the interval between paying for your outgoings and claiming for your receipts).

What is working capital?

In a manufacturing industry, once production starts, some weeks or even months must pass before the products are finished, sold, despatched and paid for. In the meantime, you must keep paying for materials, labour and overheads: the cost of all of these represents your working capital needs.

If you need to keep large stocks of raw materials or finished products or have a number of people on the payroll, materials costs and labour costs will be tied up without, for the time being, any returns. Your working capital will therefore need to be so much the greater. If your suppliers give you 30 days' credit, and your customers pay cash in seven days (in return for a small discount, perhaps), your working capital requirement will be reduced. At the same time, you will speed up your cash flow, that is, the rate at which money passes out of and into your business. Working capital and cash flow are closely related: the more money you have lying stagnant – in materials, stock, or in customers' unpaid invoices – the more working capital you will need.

In the retail and distributive trades (that is, a shop), where the goods held in stock represent the materials costs, the amount of working capital needed and the rate of cash flow depend on the amount of unsold stock, not so much on unpaid invoices because the retail trade has the advantage that customers generally pay straight away. A service industry, without stocks of materials or direct labour costs, needs comparatively little working capital: enough to pay overheads costs till the money starts coming in.

Short-term finance

As the name suggests, this is money required for short periods of time. It may be needed for start-up capital or for temporary increases in working capital.

If you are setting up a service business or an agency, or plan to be a middleman rather than a manufacturer, you may need little in the way of plant and labour, and consequently a comparatively small start-up capital. But you may still need short-term money, to cover the interval between your outgoings and your receipts.

Such short-term finance can be in the form of a loan for a stated amount, generally with a fixed interest rate and repayment date, or an overdraft. An overdraft usually has a top limit beyond which you cannot borrow; interest is calculated on a daily basis and varies according to the prevailing base rate. An overdraft is usually one of the cheapest forms of borrowing even though there may be a setting-up charge. Its great disadvantage is that it is repayable on demand – though banks seldom call it in over the short term, as timing will usually have been agreed in advance.

Medium-term finance

This is money repayable in three to seven years, and is usually needed as start-up capital to pay for plant and equipment, but it may be working capital. In the past, it was possible to borrow at a fixed rate of interest, but now, with frequent fluctuations in the base rate, a variable rate is common. The fixed-rate loan, if you can get it, is something of a gamble – you stand to lose if interest rates fall – but it does give the advantage of stability: you know exactly how much you will have to pay for your loan, which is a help in making estimates. It is generally possible to repay a loan before it is due, but check whether there are any penalties for doing so. You must, of course, be able to pay off the full amount by the stated date.

Chapter 2

Where to go for money and advice

By and large, money will always be forthcoming for a sound project if well presented. If you cannot get money for your project, either there is some flaw in it, or you have not presented it to the best advantage. If you ask your bank manager for a loan or overdraft on the basis of a few figures on the back of an envelope, you will scarcely inspire confidence.

The most obvious source of finance is a bank. Buying money is not very different from buying anything else. Banks make their profits from lending money and they want your business, provided they are sure they will not lose by it. If you approach your own bank you will have the advantage that the manager knows the state of your account; if you are generally solvent and in control of your outgoings, this will give the bank some confidence in you. You may get a rapid response, but if you do not, rather than just waiting for the answer which may turn out to be 'no', approach two or three other commercial institutions. This is probably a good idea in any case to enable you to compare the terms on offer.

Where the money may come from

If your own high-street bank refuses, try the other clearing banks, any of which may provide the finance. There are also numerous merchant banks able to provide medium-term finance. If your project is closely associated with another country, an approach to one of the country's banks might bring results.

Many banks have developed special schemes for helping new businesses: they include unsecured loan schemes, loans with capital repayment deferred and charge-free periods. It is therefore worthwhile to investigate various banks as possible sources.

How to find an investor

There are several agencies which can put you in touch with people with funds to invest.

BVCA

The BVCA (British Venture Capital Association)★ is the representative body for companies offering venture capital. Venture capital is a source of long-term finance for entrepreneurs who are ambitious to see their companies grow. Venture capital investors take a stake (generally a minority holding) in the business they invest in, but their returns are entirely dependent on the growth and profitability of the business. They want no day-to-day involvement but may want representation on the board of directors.

The BVCA publishes *A Guide to Venture Capital* to give free information on venture capital to entrepreneurs starting their own business or requiring additional capital. The guide will also help you to prepare a business plan to present when you have identified the most appropriate source of venture capital.

Members tend to invest amounts over £100,000. Their names can be found in the Association's annual directory, which lists members' investment criteria and all their contact details. You can obtain a free copy from the BVCA.

The BVCA does not make specific recommendations, so having prepared a business plan, you should approach the most appropriate source of venture capital either directly or through an adviser. You may also want to look at *Finance without Debt: A Guide to Sources of Venture Capital* (URN 96/533) published by the DTI and available from DTI Small Firms Publications.★

Business angels

Business angels are private individuals who invest, generally, in start-up businesses and in growth businesses. They tend to invest between, say, £10,000 and £250,000, often in companies close to their own homes.

The BVCA* produces a booklet listing 42 different organisations (known as Business Angel Networks or BANs), some of which are national but the majority local, which aim to match entrepreneurs to business angels. The BANs range from private companies to TECs and different BANs operate in different ways. You can obtain a copy of *Sources of Business Angel Capital* from the BVCA. Lloyds Bank publishes a guide for business owners and business angels called *Private Finance for Growing Firms*. Individual copies can be obtained free from Lloyds Bank branches.

A company may be most attractive to an angel if it meets the criteria for the Enterprise Investment Scheme (see opposite). However, angels are unlikely to invest purely on the basis of tax incentives.

LINC

LINC (Local Investment Networking Company)* is a not-for-profit organisation and one of the Business Angel Networks (see above) aiming to match entrepreneurs and potential investors. LINC has a network of 14 agencies offering a nationwide service, with the head office in London.

LINC can help you to find funding of between £10,000 and £250,000 for your business. The funds can be used either to start a business or to help your business grow. You must have a business plan. The investor will take an equity share in your business and investors usually offer managerial input too.

Businesses looking for investors are both listed in LINC's monthly Bulletin and, through a database matching service, brought to the attention of specific investors whose investment criteria they fit. The business has the opportunity to make presentations to potential investors at local meetings. A local LINC agent will look at your business plan and help prepare your entry in the Bulletin. You can contact the General Manager at the head office to be put in touch with your nearest LINC agent. LINC also provides access to other investor networks.

3i

3i plc* is a venture capital company (and member of the BVCA)* which has 18 offices throughout the UK. 3i invests in businesses across the whole business spectrum, from family firms to high-technology enterprises. It helps them at all stages of change: at start-up, when risk-capital may be required; during expansion; and later during phases of development, such as diversification, acquisition, management buy-out and management buy-in. 3i is a long-term investor which subscribes for a minority share in businesses. Its investments are usually in excess of £100,000.

Enterprise Investment Scheme (EIS)

The EIS is the successor to the Business Expansion Scheme (BES). Like its predecessor, the EIS is designed to attract individuals to invest relatively small amounts of capital in unquoted businesses. It works by giving investors tax relief when they purchase newly issued full-risk shares in an unquoted trading company. To get the full amount of tax relief, the investor must hold the shares for at least five years.

Unlike the BES, companies trading in the UK are eligible for the EIS even if they are not incorporated or resident there. Another important difference between the BES and the EIS is that investors can become paid directors of the company provided they had not been linked to the company before the shares were issued. The scheme is not open to employees or shareholders with over 30 per cent of the shares.

An investor is able to obtain income tax relief at the lower tax rate (20 per cent in 1997–8) on up to £100,000 of investment in any one tax year. If the qualifying conditions are met, the proceeds arising from the disposal of the shares after five years or more are exempt from capital gains tax. If the shares realise a loss at that time, relief against income tax or capital gains tax can be claimed.

A company can raise a maximum of £1 million through the EIS in any one tax year. A higher limit of £5 million applies to companies engaged in certain shipping activities. Note, though, that companies trading in private rented housing are specifically excluded from the EIS and in its first budget the Labour Government announced a review of the EIS to exclude other arrangements which do not carry the degree of risk that was envisaged when the scheme was introduced.

If you are in any doubt about whether your company qualifies for the EIS, you should consult your accountant or tax inspector. You may also want to look at leaflet IR137 *The Enterprise Investment Scheme* from the Inland Revenue (ask your tax office) and URN 95/806 *Enterprise Investment Scheme* from DTI Small Firms Publications.★

Other possibilities
Ask any contact you may have in the world of finance – your bank manager, accountant, stockbroker if you have one – whether they know of anybody looking for an investment. Some people have found investors by advertising in the personal columns of the daily press, but do not hope for too much with this method.

Some other sources of help

Business Link
Your nearest Business Link★ (or Business Connect★ in Wales, Business Shop★ in Scotland) is the best first port of call for information about both practical and financial help. Business Links all offer both a business information service (at little or no cost) and business advice. Pricing structures for business advice vary from one Business Link to another, but are intended to be affordable to small businesses. Typically, a personal business adviser might undertake an initial business review free of charge and from then on provide subsidised consultancy.

Enterprise agencies
The local enterprise agency is another good source of support for the small or new entrepreneur. The address and telephone number of your nearest agency can be found through your local Business Link or equivalent – see above – or in the *Yellow Pages* under 'Business enterprise agencies'.

Local enterprise agencies are supported by partnerships between local industry and local and central government. They are independent organisations, nearly all run by experienced business people, offering confidential counselling, sometimes free, to people wishing to start a business. They can advise – or, if necessary, suggest other advisers – on problems to do with the sources of finance, and with marketing, planning and training, and finding premises. They may run a number of other initiatives to support local small businesses, such as business training and seminars, small business clubs, and managed small workshop units. 'Managed' means that a manager, who may be employed by the enterprise agency or seconded from a company, attends to the letting of the units and the provision of facilities, and is also available to help and advise the tenants.

In London, the activities of LEntA,* the London Enterprise Agency, include 'Invest-a-Saturday', a one-day course broadly covering the issues surrounding setting up a business. Everyone attending the course is allocated a business adviser who will carry on giving one-to-one help afterwards. In addition seminars are offered on financial planning, bookkeeping, selling and negotiation skills, plus special design courses for London's up-and-coming designers.

LEntA is also responsible for LEntA Ventures, which is the London and home counties agent for LINC (see page 22). LEntA Ventures helps companies which are at the early stages of establishing themselves to raise small amounts of venture capital (£10,000 to £250,000) from private individuals, known as business angels.

Elsewhere in the country local enterprise agencies have developed their own programmes but offer similar types of help. In Scotland they are called enterprise trusts.

DTI Small Firms Publications

A Guide to Help for Small Firms (reference URN 97/525) is published by the DTI and contains a helpful overview of Government and other schemes designed to help small businesses. It includes information on sources of help, business services, financial help, innovation and technology and exporting and gives many useful contact addresses. You can obtain a copy from DTI Small Firms Publications.*

You may also find other DTI publications for small firms helpful. Several of these are mentioned in this chapter and the next, but you can obtain a full list of what is available from DTI Small Firms Publications. Your local Business Link* (or equivalent) should also be able to supply you with copies or help you obtain them.

Young entrepreneurs

Two organisations offer help and advice especially to young business people. The Prince's Youth Business Trust* has helped over 35,000 people aged between 18 and 30, many of them previously unemployed, to set up and run their own businesses. The Trust can provide advice and may give loans or grants to young people who have been unable to raise the finance they need elsewhere.

LiveWIRE* is supported by Shell UK Ltd and provides free local advice, information and business support to young people between 16 and 30 who are interested in setting up and running their own business. This help includes a free business start-up information pack tailored to the enquirer's specific idea, and one-to-one advice from a local business adviser. In addition, there is an annual Business Start-up Awards competition, offering cash awards and help in kind through a series of county, regional and UK events.

In addition to these two, Instant Muscle (IM)* is a charity which specialises in helping people who are unemployed and particularly disadvantaged to start their own business. It provides free assistance with all aspects of business planning on an individual basis, and up to 24 months' help after start-up, though it cannot give grants or loans.

BTG plc

BTG* identifies commercially promising technologies from universities, research institutions and companies worldwide; it then protects this technology through patents, negotiates licences with industrial partners and shares the profits with the inventors.

BTG holds over 8,500 patents and patent applications covering 250 technologies with 400 current licence agreements. Its areas of activity include pharmaceuticals, agribusiness, medical technology, automotive engineering, electronics and telecommunications. It operates internationally and has offices in the UK, the USA and Japan.

SMART

The Small Firms Merit Award for Research and Technology (SMART) is a government scheme which helps individuals and small and medium-sized businesses in England to research, design and develop technologically innovative products and processes 'for the national benefit'. SMART provides funding for two types of project: technical and commercial feasibility studies, for which grants of 75 per cent of research costs are available, up to a maximum of £45,000; and technological development projects, with grants of 30 per cent of project costs, up to a maximum of around £140,000.

You can apply for SMART at either stage of a project. However, projects must have costs of at least £30,000 for the feasibility study grants, and £60,000 for development projects. In addition, you must be able to demonstrate both that there is an element of technical risk in the project and that the grant is essential for your project to proceed. To find out more contact your local Government Office (in the phone book under 'Government') or Business Link*. For more information about help with innovative projects – or if you are outside England – contact one of the local Business and Innovation Centres whose addresses are listed in the DTI publication *A Guide to Help for Small Firms* (see page 25).

Help depending on location

For a number of years, certain areas of Britain have been designated as 'assisted areas', with various types of scheme available as means of encouraging employment. One major scheme – Regional Enterprise Grants – ended in March 1997, but another, Regional Selective Assistance, continues, and there is still government and European funding for other useful services offered locally. It is worth asking your local Business Link* what is available in your area before you embark on a project: once you have started, you may find it very hard to prove that you need help.

The Labour Government has proposed to establish a network of Regional Development Agencies in England from 1999, with the task of co-ordinating regional economic development, attracting investment in the region and supporting small businesses.

Regional Selective Assistance

This is a scheme aimed at attracting investment and encouraging employment in assisted areas, by making funding available for projects in most kinds of manufacturing industry and in some service industries. Grants of up to 15 per cent of the project costs are made, for projects such as the opening of a new plant, or modernising or improving existing sites. The sorts of thing you can get a grant for include buying plant and machinery, buying and equipping the site and some associated one-off costs, such as professional fees.

The amount of grant awarded will depend on the area, the needs of the project, the number of jobs safeguarded or created, and the impact the project will have on the economy. Note, though, that you need to demonstrate that the project would not go ahead in the same form without the grant. Further information is available from your local Business Link* or Government Office: in Scotland and Wales, contact the Scottish or Welsh Office. In Northern Ireland, similar funding may be available through LEDU.*

Presenting your case

A key prerequisite in all cases is that the proposed business must show itself likely to be viable.

For some types of finance it is stipulated that the presentation of a proposal must conform to a standard form, which may include an independent accountant's report. Each organisation has its own set of rules, so the proposal should be written to satisfy these rules. The information that the funding organisations need, and the way it is presented, should be very carefully prepared: it is almost a professional task. It is probably worth involving an accountant at some stage, if only to help review your plan before you present it and, perhaps, to help you prepare your cash flow forecast.

The bank itself may help you with a cash flow forecast: all the major banks run some form of business advisory service, free to customers, but this help is mainly intended for established businesses. However, many of the banks publish booklets intended for the person who wants to start a business. Your local Business Link* or alternative (see page 24) may also be a good source of help in creating your proposal.

Whoever helps you present your case, make sure that you, yourself, understand and believe in the assumptions and the calculations, because it is you who will have to explain and justify them to the bank manager or other potential lender, and it will be your responsibility to produce the results to match them. Your forecast must demonstrate not only that you have coherent and realistic plans for the future, but also that you will be monitoring your progress against them, week by week, month by month, and are unlikely to be overwhelmed by unforeseen disasters. The business plan is primarily for your benefit, to help you run your business properly.

What the bank manager wants to know

Make an appointment and say why you want to see the bank manager. If you are a customer, the manager will want to look up your banking record before the appointment to be assured that you can handle your money responsibly. A past overdraft will not be held against you. If you are not a customer, you will probably need to show your statements from your own bank.

The bank manager will want to know what kind of business you intend to set up; what kind and size of market you expect to trade in; the likely extent of the competition; and how you propose to go about marketing your product. He or she will ask why you consider yourself particularly qualified for this business; whether you have experience of it, for how long and with what success; and whether you have sought expert advice.

A bank manager or other potential lender will want to know exactly what resources you have, which may include redundancy money, savings, stocks and shares and other securities and investments, valuables convertible into cash; and the value of your house and car. He or she will want to know where the rest of the financing of your enterprise will come from (including other loans, perhaps a loan from a member of the family, at low interest). He or she will want to know how much you want to borrow, for how long and how you propose to pay it back, and will want to see a budget and a cash flow forecast for at least 12 months which will demonstrate that the loan can be repaid after all your business expenses have been met. See later in this chapter for information on cash flow forecasting.

The bank manager will, perhaps surprisingly, want to be sure that you are not asking for too little money. Many beginners in business are too modest in their requirements: they do not take account of all the overheads to be paid for, and forget to make provision for slack times in the trade, or unforeseen contingencies, such as a dock strike affecting export business. So, ask for what you really need and not just what you think you will get.

Offering security

The question of what security you can offer is bound to arise. A bank may lend without it, but usually only on sound propositions where it is clear that the income generated will be enough to repay the loan.

A life insurance policy is unlikely to bring in much if you surrender it to provide capital for your business, but it may be acceptable as security for a bank loan. If you own a house or other real estate, you can use it as security for a loan or overdraft, provided that it is freehold, or on a long lease (over 21 years left, say). The bank's estimate of its value will be the figure that remains after you deduct the amount owing on a first mortgage, but the bank will then probably make a further deduction to take into account what it might get on a quick sale basis. The bank will also need to ensure that anyone having an 'equitable interest' in the home (a spouse or child over 18 living in the home for instance) has taken legal advice.

An alternative to consider would be selling your house and moving to a cheaper one, or a rented one, to provide more start-up capital. If you intend to buy or rent a factory from a local authority, especially in a development area, this may secure you a high place on the housing list.

You may feel that to part with the roof over the family's head is too rash, but the people you will be asking for a loan will expect you to carry a portion of the risk. It is important to know that most financial organisations will expect your own stake in the business to equal theirs.

On the other hand, it is very easy, in the excitement of trying to raise capital for a project about which you are very enthusiastic, to give too much security to your source of finance, leaving nothing for future borrowing.

One other point: banks and other financial institutions usually make a charge for setting up a loan arrangement, generally of the order of at least 1 per cent (negotiated individually in each case). This should be allowed for in your planning calculations.

Small Firms Loan Guarantee Scheme

This is designed to assist viable small firms which are unable to raise conventional finance because of lack of security or track record. By providing a Government Guarantee against default by the borrower it enables banks and other financial institutions to lend where they would normally be unable to do so.

The guarantee would cover 85 per cent of a maximum loan of £250,000 for established businesses which have been trading for two years or more. For other businesses, the guarantee would cover 70 per cent of a maximum of £100,000. The loan term must be between 2 and 10 years. In return for providing the guarantee, the Scheme charges the customer a premium of 1.5 or 0.5 per cent of the loan amount depending on whether the loan is at a variable or fixed rate.

The Scheme is open to sole traders, partnerships, limited companies, franchises and co-operatives, but excludes some business activities, including all retailing, catering, transport business, agriculture and a number of 'intermediary' businesses, such as estate agency. The lenders have to be satisfied that they would have offered conventional finance but for the lack of security, and also that the borrower's available personal assets have all been used as security for conventional loans. The borrower may have to pledge business assets as security for the guaranteed loan. Under the Scheme rules, it is the lenders who make the commercial appraisal of all applications and the lending decision rests with them.

Several of the major participating banks operate the simplified Small Loans Arrangement which enables them to authorise loans of up to £30,000 without having to seek DTI approval first.

Full information about this scheme can be obtained via a Business Link★ or equivalent, or from the DTI Loan Guarantee Unit.★ The DTI booklet *Loan Guarantee Scheme* (URN 94/628) can be obtained from DTI Small Firms Publications.★

Mutual Guarantee Schemes

These are common in Europe and are becoming more popular in the UK as a way of allowing a number of small businesses in a region to use their collective strength to provide security for bank loans. Companies pool their savings in a 'Mutual Guarantee Society', a special form of co-operative owned and controlled by the business members. Once a fund of savings has been created, that fund is used as security to help the members to raise loans from a supporting bank, so reducing the need to give personal guarantees. The pooled savings can be used to provide a guarantee of up to 10 times the member's contribution.

To see if there is a society you can join in your area, or for information on how to set one up, contact the National Association of Mutual Guarantee Societies.★

Cash flow forecasting

At any given time there will be a difference between your outgoings and your receipts, which has to be covered from funds available in reserve, or by bank overdraft or other forms of credit.

Cash flow forecasting is calculating what this difference will be, based on month by month predictions (or educated guesses) about the times when you will be paying out and when you will be collecting money, over a period of, say, six months or a year.

The outgoings, which are largely predictable, include wages (the payment of which can never be postponed), and materials (remember that some suppliers insist on cash on delivery), VAT (which is normally paid quarterly and, if appropriate, is refunded to you quarterly) and overheads.

Your overheads will include major bills payable at different intervals: insurance once a year, rent, electricity, gas, telephone once a quarter, and so on. All these will be entered in the books as they are paid, making for an irregular pattern in your accounting, with several bills in some months, and none in others.

Receipts

The calculation of receipts is less predictable. The level of sales is likely to fluctuate from month to month. Some customers pay cash in seven days, usually expecting to be rewarded by a cash discount (negotiated in advance), others pay in 30 or 60 days (also by previous arrangement). There are bad customers and bad debts, so that part of your money may be outstanding for a long time – or forever: you should allow an estimated sum for this in each month's calculations of receipts.

It is because outgoings are more predictable than receipts that cash flow forecasting is so essential, right from the start: you may have to provide funds for wages, materials and overheads for some months during which there is little or nothing coming in.

The cash flow forecast indicates the actual movement of money, not promises to pay: it is concerned strictly with what comes in and goes out, and the time of each transaction. If you intend to raise capital by borrowing from a bank, the manager will want to examine your cash flow forecast in order to assess your ability to control your financial resources. And your bank manager will also want to see a profit and loss forecast.

How to set up a profit and loss forecast

Start by choosing a target: the amount of sales you think you can achieve in one year's time. Use as the break-even figure the minimum amount you need for your business and personal expenses, and decide how soon you have to reach that point. Not till then is the business moving into profit.

Your sales will need to increase steadily month by month in order to reach the target figure on time. Work out a set of projected monthly sales figures, and arrange them on a 12-month table.

A practical example, using manufactured products to set out the various problems, is that of Bill, a newly started small-scale manufacturer (but exactly the same method would be used for any other kind of business).

Bill, who is ambitious and confident of his market, plans to achieve sales of £50,000 a month by the end of the first year, so he plans his first year's sales as in line (1) in Table A (see overleaf).

VAT does not directly affect the calculation of business profits, so Bill disregards it in this forecast on both sales and purchases.

Bill enters in line (2) his cost of materials, which he estimates as a percentage (namely 50 per cent) of sales. He plans to use part-time labour in the first instance, building up to full-time employees as and when they can be justified. His labour figures, again a rough estimate, are expressed in line (3) as a percentage of sales (namely 30 per cent).

By subtracting the labour and materials costs from the receipts, Bill finds his monthly gross profit, in line (4).

In the case of a single-handed owner in a small service industry – say, a plumber – there would be no labour and materials costs, all expenses being charged as overheads, and the sales figures would also be the gross profit figures. In a retail or wholesale business, the materials would be the purchases of stock.

Bill knows that his overheads will vary from month to month; he is doing a one-year profit forecast, and so it is legitimate to average them over 12 months, in line (5).

The resulting set of figures in line (6) is the monthly net profit, and shows him that after the business has broken even at month 6, it is notionally trading at a profit.

Bill realises that if the business borrows money, then the interest charges will reduce the net profit, and he will need to amend the forecast.

He also realises that because he is the owner of the business as 'sole trader' (not a company), he cannot claim his monthly drawings (for his own living expenses) as a salary, that is, as part of the

Table A
Bill's projected profit and loss account (figures in £'s 000, those in square brackets are deficit)

month	1	2	3	4	5	6	7	8	9	10	11	12	Total	% of sales
(1) sales receipts	1	3	6	10	15	20	25	30	35	40	45	50	280	100
(2) *less* materials purchased	0.5	1.5	3	5	7.5	10	12.5	15	17.5	20	22.5	25	140	50
(3) *less* direct labour	0.3	0.9	1.8	3	4.5	6	7.5	9	10.5	12	13.5	15	84	30
(4) gross profit	0.2	0.6	1.2	2	3	4	5	6	7	8	9	10	56	20
(5) overheads	4	4	4	4	4	4	4	4	4	4	4	4	48	17
(6) net profit	[3.8]	[3.4]	[2.8]	[2]	[1]	–	1	2	3	4	5	6	8	3

firm's overheads. He will need to discuss his drawings with his bank manager. If he were trading as a limited company, he would pay himself a director's salary, and that would be included in the overheads.

The next step

Estimating profits is, however, only half of the story. The second, and more important half, is being in control of the cash flow. However much profit you expect to be making by the end of the first year, your estimates will be in vain if in the meantime you cannot meet your supplier's invoices, or your overhead expenses – not to mention the living expenses of you and your family.

How to set up a cash flow forecast

Table B (see overleaf) shows how Bill works out his cash flow forecast.

He reckons that he needs about £15,000 to buy plant, machinery and office furnishing. He plans to sell his present car (and lease a small van). This, with his redundancy money, means that he has some £7,000 in the bank. He has persuaded his father-in-law to let him have a further £5,000 if it is required, as a stand-by interest-free loan, to be repaid from profits.

He bases his calculations on the same 12-month scheme as his profit and loss forecast, entering his £7,000 in line (8) in the first month. It is personal capital paid into the business.

He estimates his monthly payments to suppliers in line (2): they are the materials costs from his profit forecast, and must be paid in cash, as Bill has not yet become creditworthy. He is charged VAT on these costs.

For line (3) Bill reckons that he can spread his capital payments (for plant and machinery) over the first six months during which time he will be building up his sales. He is charged VAT on these purchases.

Wages and salaries (including National Insurance contributions) in line (4) must be paid promptly.

For the purpose of costing, the overheads were averaged out per unit of product, but they cannot be averaged out in making a cash flow forecast: the bills come in and have to be paid at irregular

Table B
Bill's projected cash flow (figures in £'s 000, those in square brackets are deficit)

month	1	2	3	4	5	6	7	8	9	10	11	12	13
(1) opening bank balance/ overdraft	nil	[2.18]	[10.72]	[19.9]	[26.08]	[30.58]	[38.58]	[47.71]	[46.14]	[46.13]	[53.02]	[47.14]	[42.14]
PAYMENTS (inc VAT)													
(2) suppliers	0.59	1.76	3.53	5.88	8.81	11.75	14.69	17.63	20.56	23.5	26.44	29.38	29.38
(3) plant and machinery	2.35	5.88	2.35	1.18	2.35	3.53							
(4) wages and salaries (inc NI)	0.3	0.9	1.8	3.0	4.5	6.0	7.5	9.0	10.5	12.0	13.5	15.0	15.0
(5) overheads with VAT	2.94	1.18	3.53	0.59				1.18	1.18		1.18		
no VAT	8.0		1.5	5.0		2.0	8.0	3.0	3.0	5.0		3.5	8.0
(6) VAT office							2.44			7.52			11.63
(7) maximum borrowing requirement	[14.18]	[11.9]	[23.43]	[34.96]	[42.33]	[56.21]	[71.21]	[75.52]	[81.38]	[94.15]	[94.14]	[95.02]	[106.15]
RECEIPTS (inc VAT)													
(8) capital – Bill	7.0												
– family loan	5.0												
(9) sales	–	1.18	3.53	7.05	11.75	17.63	23.5	29.38	35.25	41.13	47.0	52.88	58.75
(10) VAT office				1.83									
Closing bank balance													
(11) projected borrowing	[2.18]	[10.72]	[19.9]	[26.08]	[30.58]	[38.58]	[47.71]	[46.14]	[46.13]	[53.02]	[47.14]	[42.14]	[47.40]

intervals, and this is reflected in line (5). VAT will be charged on some overheads (e.g. advertising, stationery) but not on others (e.g. rent and rates). Bill includes the appropriate amounts.

It is obvious to Bill that he will need his father-in-law's loan, so he includes it in line (8).

Bill next goes to line (9) and fills in his sales figures (including VAT), but, as he is giving a month's credit, his first cash receipts come in month 2. He now deals with VAT in lines (6) and (10). He totals the VAT charged against the business in each quarter: against this he sets the corresponding amounts which he has charged against his customers. But the VAT office (HM Customs and Excise) does not recognise the one month's credit he gives to his customers so, for VAT purposes, Bill must carry back the sales receipt figures to the month before: e.g., the sales credited in month 2 represent a VAT receipt in month 1, in which the goods were invoiced and delivered. In months 1–3, more VAT has been charged against the business than the business has charged, so Bill gets a refund from the VAT office in month 4 (line 10). The case is altered in the subsequent quarters, and Bill has to pass on the excess received to the VAT office, line (6).

Bill now looks at the cash flow month by month. For month 1, the total of payments which is the maximum borrowing requirement (line 7), exceeds both his capital and the family loan (line 8), leaving the business with an overdraft of £2,180 (line 1). He carries this forward as the opening figure in line (1) for month 2. By the end of month 2, the overdraft has increased to £10,720, even with the receipts from the first month's sales. This, too, is carried forward to line (1) for month 3, and so on, month by month. Bill's borrowing requirement, line (11), increases and, at the end of the year, his overdraft is over £42,000, and has been even higher than this for the previous five months.

Bill is startled to find that he needs such heavy borrowing to achieve a profit of £8,000 (net, but before interest payments) for the year. This is daunting; he notices that the borrowing drops after reaching a peak in month 10, and this looks to be a promising trend. To check this, he adds a month 13 projection, keeping purchases from suppliers steady at the month 12 level. Alas, he finds that his overdraft increases again because of the VAT payment he has to make in this month. He then looks to see if there are any overheads which he can re-time, or delay paying, but finds that this makes no significant difference to his business.

To improve his forecasts, Bill looks at ways of reducing all outgoings. He accepts that reduced purchases of materials will necessarily reduce sales. He fixes on a less ambitious monthly sales figure of £40,000, but aims for a faster growth in sales, so that he will achieve that figure in month 10, and break even in month 5. By leasing instead of buying some of the plant and machinery he can reduce his capital cash expenditure, but will incur leasing charges, on which VAT is payable. He needs to re-time some of the outgoings, but feels it would be unwise to reduce them all.

Bill now amends his profit and loss forecast, and his cash flow forecast, as shown in Tables C and D. Table C shows profits only £200 lower, and Table D shows reduced borrowing from month 7. The year-end overdraft is now £23,250, nearly £19,000 down on his first forecast. He finds that in month 13 the overdraft increases, but is still nearly £18,000 down on the original forecast.

The new forecasts, like the old ones, do not provide for interest on borrowing, or for Bill's personal drawings. None of them answers the question: 'When can you repay the loan?' which the lenders are sure to ask. Bill does a back-of-the-envelope extension forecast to month 24: he assumes no changes in purchases and sales, wages, overheads, etc., and ignores inflation. He realises that this is very rough and ready and unrealistic, but still, by showing the cash flow in credit for the last few months, it is a pointer to the sort of term which Bill needs for his borrowing, i.e. 3–5 years, rather than 15–20 years.

Bill believes that the new forecasts can be met, and that they can serve as the foundation of a preliminary talk with the bank manager. After that, they will have to be worked up, probably with professional help, before being presented to the bank or to other possible lenders. Bill will need to be able to set out clearly the assumptions behind any estimated figures in the cash flow forecast.

Not borrowing but leasing

Leasing is a form of getting medium-term finance without the need to borrow money. The plant, equipment and vehicles you need are bought by the lessor (who may be a finance company) and then

Table C
Bill's amended projected profit and loss account (figures in £'s 000, those in square brackets are deficit)

month	1	2	3	4	5	6	7	8	9	10	11	12	Total	% of sales
(1) sales receipts less VAT	3	6	10	15	20	25	30	35	35	40	40	40	299	100
(2) less materials purchased	1.5	3	5	7.5	10	12.5	15	17.5	17.5	20	20	20	149.5	50
(3) less direct labour	0.9	1.8	3	4.5	6	7.5	9	10.5	10.5	12	12	12	89.7	30
(4) gross profit	0.6	1.2	2	3	4	5	6	7	7	8	8	8	59.8	20
(5) overheads	4	4	5	4	4	5	4	4	5	4	4	5	52	17.3
(6) net profit	[3.4]	[2.8]	[3]	[1]	–	–	2	3	2	4	4	3	7.8	2.7

Table D
Bill's amended projected cash flow (figures in £'s 000, those in square brackets are deficit)

month	1	2	3	4	5	6	7	8	9	10	11	12	13
(1) opening bank balance/ overdraft	nil	[4.54]	[8.7]	[19.59]	[26.72]	[28.60]	[30.47]	[40.35]	[36.75]	[32.04]	[39.72]	[30.57]	[23.25]
PAYMENTS (inc VAT)													
(2) suppliers	1.76	3.53	5.88	8.81	11.75	14.69	17.63	20.56	20.56	23.5	23.5	23.5	23.5
(3) plant and machinery	2.35	1.18	2.35	1.18									
(4) wages and salaries (inc NI)	0.9	1.8	3.0	4.5	6.0	7.5	9.0	10.5	10.5	12.0	12.0	12.0	12.0
(5) overheads – with VAT	3.53	1.18	3.53		1.76			0.59	1.18		2.35	1.18	
– no VAT	8.0		2.0	5.0		2.0	8.0		3.0	5.0		3.0	8.0
– leasing			1.18			1.18			1.18			1.18	
(6) VAT office							4.63			8.31			9.97
(7) maximum borrowing requirement	[16.54]	[12.23]	[26.64]	[39.08]	[46.23]	[53.97]	[69.73]	[72.0]	[73.17]	[80.85]	[77.57]	[70.25]	[76.72]
RECEIPTS (inc VAT)													
(8) capital – Bill	7.0												
– family loan	5.0												
(9) sales	–	3.53	7.05	11.75	17.63	23.5	29.38	35.25	41.13	41.13	47.0	47.0	47.0
(10) VAT office				0.61									
Closing bank balance													
(11) projected borrowing	[4.54]	[8.7]	[19.59]	[26.72]	[28.60]	[30.47]	[40.35]	[36.75]	[32.04]	[39.72]	[30.57]	[23.25]	[29.72]

leased to you for an agreed rent. At the end of the contract it is common for the leased equipment to be sold, and the greatest part of the proceeds (say 90 per cent) will then be returned to you as a rebate of rentals; or you may be able to continue leasing the equipment at a reduced rental.

The lessor claims any tax allowances (such as capital allowances) that may be available, and this is reflected in the level of rental charges, which would otherwise be higher. You yourself can offset the whole rental against tax, although there may be a ceiling on the amount you can deduct for the rental of 'expensive' cars (with a purchase price in excess of £12,000).

The main advantage of leasing is that your working capital is not tied up in rapidly depreciating machinery and you can reduce your borrowing needs.

The first approach to the lessor generally has to come from you, the potential lessee (though some manufacturers, e.g. of office equipment, practise 'sales aid leasing' – the salesman approaches you fully prepared to arrange a lease). If you are new to the lessor, you may be required to establish your creditworthiness, for example by providing a bank reference, but usually no security other than the leased goods is required; you may be asked to pay a few months' rental in advance. You have to specify exactly what equipment you want and, if the deal is approved, the lessor buys it from the manufacturer and leases it to you on the agreed terms.

Vehicles and some office equipment can sometimes be leased for short periods and exchanged later for more up-to-date models, but you need to check your contract carefully to see whether this would be possible and on what terms. If you are leasing the kind of equipment which requires regular servicing you may be offered a 'service-inclusive' contract. You should compare the terms offered for this with any available alternatives for separate leases and service contracts.

Many major providers of lease finance to industry and commerce in the UK are members of the Finance & Leasing Association.* You can ask for a list of members to be sent to you. Most of them are London-based but operate in any part of the country. The Association also produces an annual report which gives an overview of the types of leasing business undertaken by members.

Hire-purchase is another way of obtaining plant and equipment without capital outlay. Just as in domestic purchases, you pay a deposit and then regular fixed instalments, and at the end of the contract you are given the option to pay a further fee, upon which the goods become your property. The instalment payments are generally higher than interest on a bank loan, but you may not wish to, or be able to, increase your bank loan. The counterbalancing advantage is that in a hire-purchase agreement the terms are normally fixed, so that the charges cannot be increased if interest rates generally should rise (although you may find variable rate deals for larger amounts).

Two DTI booklets, *A Guide to Hire Purchase and Leasing* (URN 95/684) and *Money and Machines* (URN 95/555) are available from DTI Small Firms Publications★ and DTI Publications Orderline★ respectively, or from the Finance & Leasing Association.

Looking at the figures

Bill's case has several vital lessons for the new entrepreneur. First of all, you will certainly be surprised when you discover just how much money you are going to need as working capital. It is easy to underestimate one's requirements. Many businesses which are expanding make that mistake: they run out of money because they expand too rapidly. This is called overtrading.

Secondly, an estimated profit margin may appear ample, yet if the volume of sales turns out to be lower than the forecast, the total profits may fail to cover outgoings.

Nearly every first attempt at a profit and loss forecast is too ambitious. That is why a cash flow forecast is needed: to warn the small businessman or businesswoman when resources are not equal to ambitions.

It is easy to recast figures at the planning stage in order to deploy one's resources to best advantage, and arrive at a satisfactory and realistic forecast which can confidently be put before a bank or other financial organisation. However, it is terribly easy, when you have produced a forecast you do not like, to adjust the assumptions and figures – in that order – so that it all looks workable. You must look at original assumptions and new ones and see if you are not introducing too much wishful thinking.

Why you will need an accountant

If you already know something about business accounting and revel in figures, you may think that you can do without an accountant.

Bear in mind, though, that however nimble with numbers you may be, you are unlikely to have an accountant's grasp of the innumerable regulations relating to taxation or the relevant aspects of company and revenue law, nor his or her experience in dealing with the Board of Inland Revenue, nor the all-round familiarity with different aspects of business. Here are some of the problems with which an accountant can help you:

- to decide whether to set up as a sole trader, partnership or a limited company
- to find ways of raising capital
- to set up cash flow forecasts and profit and loss forecasts
- to decide whether to register for VAT if you do not have to
- to choose a starting date, and more important still, a trading year-end date
- to keep day-to-day records, account books and ledgers
- to claim all possible allowances, expenses and reliefs against tax, and to negotiate with the tax inspector
- to fill in your tax return under the new system of self-assessment
- to cope with pensions, annuities and insurance.

Choosing an accountant must be done carefully. It is necessary to make sure that someone has proper qualifications (look for the letters FCA or ACA after someone's name). For tax advice, look for the letters ATII or FTII, denoting members of the Chartered Institute of Taxation.* Use the *Yellow Pages* to find names and addresses. If you want a full list of chartered accountants practising in your area, contact your local District Society of Chartered Accountants (in the phone book under 'Accountants').

For more information contact The Institute of Chartered Accountants in England and Wales.* It publishes several useful booklets, including *Mind Your Own Business*, *Choosing a Chartered Accountant* and *Why You Need a Chartered Accountant*.

Chapter 3

How are you going to trade?

You will have to decide whether to trade as a sole trader, in a partnership, or as a limited company. A co-operative is a much less usual business form, but may also be worth considering. You can usually change to another legal entity later, as your business develops.

Deciding how to trade should be an integral part of your plans, and is something that you should discuss with your professional adviser. There are various considerations, and some which might be significant for your business could be quite unimportant for another. The Lawyers For Your Business★ scheme provides a free half-hour consultation with a participating solicitor.

As to considerations of taxation, what you must do is compare the trading position of a sole trader or partnership and that of a company; and also compare your own position as a sole trader or partner, with your position as a shareholder-owner and salaried director of a limited company. You have to decide what aspects of taxation are most important for you.

For instance, some businesses are likely, in their early years, to make losses which are useful for tax purposes. If you are trading as a company, these losses can be carried forward and set against profits in future years. If you are a sole trader (or partnership), you can do this too, but there is also scope for carrying the losses sideways, and setting them against any other income you may receive, and scope for carrying them back to earlier years.

The choice may not be clear-cut, but you should try to assess where the balance of advantage lies. Circumstances may change, so you should periodically review your choice. It is usually possible to change from sole trader (or partnership) to a company without too many tax snags: changing the other way is more difficult.

Sole trader

Being a sole trader does not mean you have to work alone, but that you are totally and solely responsible for the business. You take all the profits, but you are also personally liable for all the debts incurred to the full extent of your means. Should you not have the money in the business to pay your business debts, your personal possessions, including your home, could be taken in settlement.

Many small businesses start as sole traders and are later turned into limited companies.

Partnership

A business partnership is an association of two or more people (up to 20) trading together as one firm and sharing the profits. The partners are normally 'jointly and severally' liable for the whole of the firm's debts, to the full extent of their personal means, just as though they were a sole trader. This means that if one partner should abscond, the others have to pay all the outstanding debts, including what would have been the absconder's share.

An exception to the normal 'joint and several' rule for debts applies to tax (but not VAT). From 6 April 1997, partnership tax has no longer been a joint and several liability. The partnership as a whole gets a tax return, but the partners must each enter their own share of pre-tax profit on their own tax return, and are then responsible for paying the tax in the same way as if they were sole traders.

It is possible to set up limited partnerships, with each partner's liability being limited to the amount of capital contributed, but such partnerships must have at least one partner who is fully liable for the firm's debts and must register with Companies House★ (see 'Formalities', page 47). In addition, limited partners cannot take part in the management of the business.

It is important, in a partnership, to have a simple agreement, drawn up by a solicitor and setting out each partner's share of the profits, and how each partner's share is to be valued if he or she wants to withdraw from the partnership, or a new partner comes in; and, if one of the partners dies, what should happen to his or her share.

The agreement should state for how long the partnership is to run or under what conditions it can be terminated. Partnerships that go sour can be messy and upsetting, so it is wise to lay down guidelines of who does what and what should happen in the case of a dispute. Other points that must be agreed are: how much can each partner draw (e.g. monthly) on account of his or her share of the profit? Are there equal voting rights? Who signs the cheques? What are the arrangements for holidays, and what happens in the case of long illness? What happens if an ex-partner wants to start trading in competition?

All the partners may work in the firm; or one or more of them may be 'sleeping partners' who just put in money. A partnership agreement can include any clauses specific to the particular set of circumstances.

Sole traders and partnerships may trade under their own name or names, or else under another name or title. However, if the name that you have chosen to trade under is not your own surname(s), you must indicate the name(s) of the owner(s) on all stationery, and display them in your shop or office or place of work.

Limited company

A limited company is a legal entity, just as though it were a person, and must be conducted according to the rules laid down by company law. They include the maintenance of accounts, an annual audit, and the disclosure of the company's activities to the general public. However, some of the requirements are relaxed for smaller companies. In particular, there is no requirement for an annual audit if your annual turnover is £350,000 or less.

The shareholder(s) (there need only be one) are the owners of the company, but are liable for its debts only to the extent of the face value of their shares. However, a director's liability can be extended by personal guarantees that he or she may have given to a bank or other financial institution as security for a business loan. Under the 1986 Insolvency Act, directors are made personally liable and subject to criminal prosecution if they continue trading or take credit knowing that the company is insolvent.

Limited companies may be public or private. If public ('plc'), the shares may be made available to the general public and may be quoted on the Stock Exchange. Private companies – which are the majority – do not offer shares to the public, and style themselves 'Limited' or 'Ltd'.

Formalities

You can obtain the DTI publication *Setting Up in Business: A Guide to Regulatory Requirements* (URN 97/524) from DTI Small Firms Publications.★

Limited companies must be registered with Companies House★ in Cardiff (for England and Wales), Companies House★ in Edinburgh (for Scotland) and the Companies Registry★ in Belfast (for Northern Ireland).

Registration entails submitting a memorandum of association which must include details of the name of the company, its country of registration, the objects of the company, a statement of the limited liability of its members, the amount of share capital and how it is divided into shares. It must be properly signed and witnessed.

You may also submit articles of association (which is something different from the memorandum). They cover a variety of internal matters: broadly speaking, they deal with the rights and powers of the directors and the members; meetings; votes; issue of new shares and restrictions on transfer of shares, such as the right of first refusal for the other members if one of them wishes to dispose of his or her shares. It is very often easiest simply to say that the standard articles under the Companies Act will apply, and then to list such alterations and additions to them as suit one's particular circumstances.

Other forms to be completed on registration cover: details of (and consent to act by) first directors and secretary; precise address of the company's registered office; and a statutory declaration that all the formalities have been complied with.

The fees payable on registration are as follows: £20 for a new incorporation; £10 for a change of company name; and £15 a year thereafter, for filing the company's annual return with the Registrar of Companies. A same-day service for registration or change of company name is available: the current fee is £100.

It is important to have professional help in registering a company. Some lawyers and accountants specialise in this.

Also, there are company registration agents, through whom you can 'buy' a company off the shelf. The agent has registered the company with stand-in directors, shareholders and secretary, but the company is not operating. When you buy the company, your names are substituted for those of the stand-ins.

If you buy a ready-made company set-up, its name may not be to your liking, but you can change this through Companies House.

Your choice of trading name must conform to the rules laid down by the Companies Act 1985 and the Business Names Act 1985 – in Northern Ireland, the Business Names (Northern Ireland) Order 1986 – which are designed to enable anyone dealing with a business to know the owner's name and address. They amount, briefly, to this: the owner of a business must disclose his or her surname (if a sole trader) or surnames (if it is a partnership) or full corporate name (if it is a limited company), together with the address in each case, on the business premises and stationery, if he or she chooses to trade under some name other than the surname(s) or corporate name. So, for example, if you trade as R. Random, or (Roderick) Random and (Humphrey) Clinker, or Peregrine Pickles Ltd., you are not affected, but formulations such as 'Random's Travel Service', or 'The Perfect Pickle' will require compliance with the disclosure rules. A complete explanation of these and other rules relating to business names is available in *Notes for Guidance on Business Names and Business Ownership* from the Registrar of Companies.

Co-operative

A co-operative is a business enterprise which is jointly owned by its members. A *worker co-operative* is owned and controlled by its employees; a *consumer co-operative* by its customers; a *community co-operative* by the community which the co-operative serves; a *service* or *secondary co-operative* by the users of the services provided (such as a group of small businesses collectively owning and managing their premises).

A co-operative may take various forms including co-ownership, in which case, when the co-operative winds up, members can divide any surplus over liabilities among themselves; or it may be a common ownership, in which case, on winding up, any surplus will be donated to another, similar, co-operative.

A co-operative may be registered under the Industrial and Provident Societies Acts, with members having limited liability, or it may be incorporated as a limited company. An I & PS co-operative founded by individuals must always have at least three members; a limited company co-operative needs only two members.

Most new co-operatives register either as an I & PS or as a company limited by guarantee, sometimes using one of the sets of model rules available from promoting bodies such as ICOM★ (Industrial Common Ownership Movement), or EOS★ (Employee Ownership Scotland). Model rules make registration easier, cheaper and quicker than having a constitution drawn up, but promoting bodies can provide a 'tailor-made' service on request. EOS and ICOM also have model rules for companies limited by shares which can participate in the Enterprise Investment Scheme. Costs can vary between the different agencies and the different legal structures.

The registration process takes between two and eight weeks – though much longer if any queries should arise. Adopting the model rules, which are already approved by the Registrar, helps to prevent this.

The essence of a co-operative is that it is run for the benefit of its members and has a democratic constitution: everyone who qualifies may become a member and, generally, has one vote, irrespective of the size of his or her investment. This does not mean that every issue is put to the vote: while very small co-operatives may involve all the members in day-to-day management matters, most of the 2,500 or so registered co-operatives delegate these powers to an elected committee, which remains accountable to the membership. Few worker co-operatives employ a paid manager in the conventional sense of the word, but it is common in other cooperatives.

A co-operative must, of course, be commercially viable if it is to survive and compete with other enterprises, and must be conducted on proper business lines. However, when profits are generated, members decide what proportion of the surplus should go to reserves, and what proportion should be distributed among members, usually depending on the extent to which they have traded with or taken part in the business of the society. And though a co-operative may not need to produce a dividend, it must still be able to meet its interest payments and capital repayments on loans.

The principle of co-operation may help to keep the enterprise afloat where ordinary companies would founder. For instance, during difficult trading times members may be willing to reduce their expectations and even make some sacrifices for the good of the whole organisation.

Co-operatives may start in different ways. Most are new-start businesses, but some are formed by workers or members of the community to take over existing businesses, including ones which have failed in the hands of conventional management. This last option, the so-called 'phoenix' co-operative, is by no means simple, and though the attempt may attract much publicity, in most cases it will be possible only if the original business is scaled down considerably before being revived as a co-operative.

New-start co-operatives are created by groups of individuals who wish to combine their skills or pursue a common interest to create a democratically controlled business; or by members of a community (which may be a geographical community or a 'community of interest') who create a co-operative to provide themselves with a service that they need; or by small businesses that wish to own and manage collectively resources needed by all, such as premises or marketing.

If you are considering establishing your business as a co-operative, you will need specialist advice. Most areas of the country are served by either a local Co-operative Development Agency, or by local authority officers with specific responsibility for co-operatives. If neither of these facilities is available to you, or you do not know how to contact them, ICOM (see below) will be able to advise you.

Getting Help

Among the places to go for help or information are:

Industrial Common Ownership Movement (ICOM)*

ICOM promotes and advises worker co-operatives and other forms of employee ownership; provides specialist registration and legal services for co-operatives and community enterprises; offers training and consultancy services; has an extensive mail-order catalogue of publications; can assist in raising money from Europe for co-operative training schemes; and provides legal, technical and practical services to its members. Membership is open to all co-operatives, support organisations and sympathisers.

Industrial Common Ownership Finance Limited (ICOF)*

ICOF administers a revolving loan fund on a national basis for co-operative and community enterprises. It also has specific loan funds for particular areas of the country.

Loans are generally from £5,000 to £50,000 over five years at an interest rate typically between 10 and 12 per cent. Enterprises which apply for such loans must be able to demonstrate their co-operative status, and also their commercial viability.

Registry of Friendly Societies*

The Registry is the government department which gives information about rules and registration and is responsible for registering Industrial and Provident Societies. The Registry of Friendly Societies in London currently deals with England and Wales, while the Edinburgh one deals with Scotland, but from some point in 1999 friendly societies will become the responsibility of the Financial Services Authority. Such societies in Northern Ireland come under the wing of the Registry of Credit Unions and Industrial and Provident Societies* in Belfast.

Employee Ownership Scotland (EOS)*

This organisation offers guidance to groups of people wishing to form employee-owned businesses including co-operatives. Such advice covers all forms of business consultancy and there is now a loan fund available to provide capital requirements for new and existing co-operatives in the whole of Scotland.

Management buy-outs

A lot of publicity has been given in recent years to employees buying the business in which they work. This is, in fact, an opportunity which arises only rarely; the owner's motives for selling the business (and, of course, the accounts of the business) should be scrutinised very carefully.

If you are planning to buy a business which has failed, then unless you know exactly why the original company went out of business, and have definite proposals for putting things right, you will not find it easy to raise the necessary finance.

If you have been made redundant by the winding up of a company or know of a company that has been wound up, consider whether there is any part of the operation or assets (some of the workshop plant, for instance) that you could buy and use in starting a project of your own.

There is little to stop employees who leave an existing company from setting up in competition. Even if there is a clause in their contract of employment restricting their future business ventures, the courts will not uphold a contract that is a restraint of trade and denies anyone the right to earn a living. However, the ex-employer may stop former employees from making use of his or her trade secrets or confidential information by taking out an injunction.

Always be cautious, and make sure you do not overcommit yourself financially.

Franchises

The principle involved in franchising is basically this: a company which is successful in manufacturing a product or providing a service decides to extend its activities nationally or internationally. Instead of setting up its own company-owned branches, it becomes a franchisor, selling its experience and established reputation to individuals, the franchisees.

Franchises – a ready-made business identity

The purchase of a franchise is the purchase of the right to use a particular method to run a particular kind of business. You are buying expertise and an image, sometimes the right to use and trade under a household name. The entry price can be considerable – it is for you to assess whether the potential rewards are commensurate.

Becoming a franchisee usually means that you will own the business assets (premises, equipment and so on) – although some franchisors prefer to own the business premises and lease them to franchisees. But you will certainly not own the business method. You are at liberty to decide the most appropriate method of trading, whether as a sole trader, in partnership or through a limited company.

A vast array of over 500 franchises can be purchased. These range from the fast food industry (Wimpy, KFC) to service industries (Prontaprint, Dyno-Rod). In acquiring a franchise, you are able to run your own business and still be part of a large network.

However, your business operation, and your trading accounts in particular, will be subject to scrutiny by a (it is to be hoped, reasonably benevolent) Big Brother. As the franchisor will have spent time and money developing the business, you will be subject to controls as to how the business is operated. In order to enable the franchisor to monitor the network and analyse the results, there will also be certain obligations imposed upon you with regard to the trading accounts, and the reporting procedures between you and the franchisor.

You must be very clear from the outset about one point: you will be buying a right to trade for a limited period only, typically five years. This may be coupled with the right to renew the franchise at the end of that period. The cost to you will be the payment of a capital sum on entering into the agreement, and probably also further sums (service fees) while the agreement lasts. The latter may be related to sales or turnover, or both.

While you will need to vet thoroughly any prospective franchisor, you must expect also to be vetted by it; indeed, the better the organisation you are thinking of joining, the more concerned it is likely to be to ensure that only franchisees of high calibre are taken on. So you will each need to make a good impression on the other.

The clearing banks have specialised departments that deal with, and advise on, franchises. Understandably they take the view that the purchase of a suitable franchise helps to minimise the risks of starting up a business. You will, of course, need to make your own capital contribution to the initial costs; a bank will generally expect this to be at least 30 per cent of the total. Subject to this point, the raising of capital will be likely to be more straightforward than in starting a business from scratch.

How does the franchising system work?
There are no hard and fast rules, because the diversity of businesses and business ideas inevitably gives rise to very different systems.

At the core of the agreement will be an operations manual incorporating the essential business techniques which you, as franchisee, are obliged to use. Expect a franchisor to stipulate exactly what accounting systems you are to use (he or she will need uniformity among franchisees since he or she will be inspecting their accounts and may want to draw management information from them); and how you are required to run the business. Opening hours may be stipulated; in the case of a shop, the franchisor may retain complete control over the décor and furnishings and training of staff. The particular methods and techniques of, for example, preparing and cooking the food in a fast food chain may be laid down – you may, in this case, be obliged to buy certain foodstuffs and ingredients only from the franchisor. The operations manual is, of course, a confidential document and its contents, trade secrets and knowhow must not be revealed.

You will be required by the franchisor to enter into a contract (a franchise agreement). You should take professional advice on this and will need to understand how it deals with issues such as:

- The initial training to be provided by the franchisor. This should provide you with the requisite skills to run the business efficiently. This is part of what you are buying with your initial capital sum.
- The level of back-up which the franchisor is obliged to provide, such as advertising and general promotion, advice and trouble-shooting. This is, in effect, the return which you get for the service fees charged. The franchisor is entitled to a profit. Similarly, you are entitled to an efficient back-up service from him or her and ought to know that there is an obligation to spend money for the good of the network of franchisees and to continue to take an interest in it.
- What goods and provisions you are obliged to buy through the franchisor, and what controls there are over the price which he or she charges for them.
- Whether you have exclusive trading rights as franchisee in a defined geographical area. This is generally regarded as one of the key elements of a franchise.
- How long the franchise runs, and on what terms it is renewable.
- Whether any restrictions on trading will affect you when the franchise comes to an end.
- Whether the continuation of the franchise is dependent on a minimum level of turnover or profit or any other factors. (When you have parted with what may have been a sizeable capital sum, it would be fairly disastrous if the franchise could be withdrawn unfairly.)
- What will happen if you want (or are obliged) to sell the business. The better franchisors are likely to insist on complete control over the vetting of any new franchisee, so your ability to sell as a

going concern may be dependent on the franchisor's goodwill and/or the quality of the prospective buyer. The potential problem here is that of being left with only the shell of a business to sell, but no goodwill. One solution would be to insist that the franchisor is obliged to purchase the business from you if no other satisfactory franchisee can be found to step into your shoes.

However, most franchisors use standard forms of franchise agreement and are not prepared to allow significant changes to them. The justification offered is the need for uniformity in business operations.

Some words of warning

For a franchise to be successful, it needs to combine a successful business idea with a proper level of support and promotion from the franchisor. If a capital sum is payable for an exclusive right to distribute goods or offer a certain service within a given area, but no back-up is offered, think hard whether you could set up a similar operation yourself and perhaps save a great deal of money.

Cowboy franchisors also exist. They charge a relatively high buy-in fee but offer little or no training or equipment. Or the sum involved may be low – about £5,000, say, which is modest by ethical franchising standards – but when you look into what you would be getting for this, you may realise that there is very little tangible return.

The most tell-tale sign of a franchisor who is not above-board is that he or she demands an excessively high franchise fee and management service fee. Ten per cent of turnover is average, though some franchisors may set a somewhat higher rate, in return for providing special facilities for franchisees; but anything grossly in excess of this should be regarded with suspicion unless it is matched by a demonstrably high level of support.

Unscrupulous cowboy franchisors are happy to take your money for what at first sight seems a sound business idea, but if you do not end up with a distinctive product or service to offer, you should leave well alone. Be sure to have any potential franchise agreement thoroughly vetted by your solicitor, and the financial side of the undertaking by your accountant. You will need to establish:

* Whether the franchisor is a member of the British Franchise Association (see below). A member is bound by a code of ethics designed to protect franchisees.

- What experiences other franchisees have had. A reputable franchisor cannot have grounds to refuse a request for a list of its franchisees.

Finally, ask yourself this question: if the business idea is such a money-spinner, why is the franchisor not running the business – or is it the sale of the franchise that is the true money-spinner?

A good business idea or method can warrant a substantial capital sum. In taking on a franchise you will become a partner – but probably only a second-class one – in a business, and certainly the partner undertaking financial risk. You must decide whether the degree of outside control warrants extra financial commitment.

It is best to deal with a franchisor who is a member of the British Franchise Association.* The BFA has published a Franchisee Guide (£25 including postage and packing). You can obtain the DTI publication, *An Introduction to Franchising* (URN 96/999), by contacting DTI Small Firms Publications.*

Buying an existing business

The purchase of an existing business is usually undertaken by people who are already in business and wish to expand their operations or change business venues. But it makes equally sound economic sense for someone starting in business to acquire an established niche in a market. The main impediment is likely to be cost.

The extra items for which you will have to pay on acquiring an established business are:

Stock
When starting a business from scratch, you have time in which to build up your customer base, and your stock level at inception will probably be a moderate one. By contrast, the value of the stock of some types of existing business may exceed the aggregate cost of the premises and goodwill.

Trade fittings
Business premises need furniture and other items of equipment and fittings – in a shop, these will include shelving, cash tills and perhaps freezers, etc., all of which must be bought from the seller.

Goodwill – the indispensable aspect of business

A flourishing business is worth more than the sum of its constituent parts. The difference between the two is called goodwill, the value of which is affected principally by the turnover of the business. This is an oversimplification, since the value of the business is also affected by the figures attributed to items such as leases and fittings for the purposes of accounting and tax.

The term 'goodwill' is used here as a general designation to cover customer loyalty and all other intangible (mainly external) factors which give a business its status and enable it to run profitably. It means different things in different businesses.

As a prospective buyer of an established business, you will need to satisfy yourself as far as possible that the goodwill exists and will continue to exist after you take it over. This is a tall order. Some of the factors which make the difference between success and failure are intangible, and are much more likely to be perceived by someone with previous business experience. But a commonsense approach and a sceptical stance will take you a long way to understanding the essentials of a business. Professional advice from an accountant and a solicitor experienced in business should not be dispensed with. Their investigations should bring to light any serious problems affecting the business.

An accountant's job is to scrutinise the business accounts. These will rarely tell the whole truth. However, they ought to contain sufficient of the truth to tell him or her how the business is structured financially, and from this your accountant will be able to calculate your financial requirements and to let you know whether you stand a chance of making a go of it. For example, a business from which the proprietor makes a comfortable living but on which there are no outstanding bank loans may be a potentially lethal trap for the buyer who needs to borrow heavily. The two proprietors have entirely different financial requirements. An experienced accountant should also be able to judge, from knowledge of other similar businesses, whether the accounts suggest that the business you wish to buy differs in any important way from other such businesses. Unfortunately, there is no safeguard against an unscrupulous seller who falsifies his or her accounts, other than perhaps your instinct and that of the people advising and helping you.

A solicitor will advise you on the purchase contract, and the initial enquiries may bring in important information.

Local authority search and enquiries

These do not tell as much about a property and its locality as people generally suppose. Apart from road proposals affecting land within 200 metres of the property, a local authority search will only give information about the property itself: the effect of planning legislation, compulsory purchase or demolition orders, liability for road works, financial orders and other matters which could affect it. But the search will not provide information about other property.

So, if the next-door property is due to be demolished to make way for a hypermarket, you and your solicitor will not necessarily be any the wiser from reading the result of a local search. As part of the search process, you can ask for information about planning applications for property in the vicinity, but local authorities have their own guidelines for how much information they will provide in this way.

However, you are entitled to inspect the planning register at the local authority offices. There you can read the planning history of all properties in the neighbourhood and also see what applications have been lodged but not yet decided on. You can also talk to the planning officials about local trends and developments. Look out for pointers to help you assess the future prospects of a business, such as:

- new housing in the neighbourhood – will this bring potential new customers?
- the diversion of a road, or the construction of a bypass – will this adversely affect passing trade or your accessibility to your customers?
- creation of a pedestrian precinct (which tends to boost trade for shops within the precinct) – might it perhaps draw trade away from businesses outside it?

Remember that planning permission is required for a property to be used for business purposes. You need to check (with your solicitor's help if necessary) that the premises have got the appropriate planning permission. If you think the nature of your business might change, this could call for a planning application.

Enquiries of the seller's solicitor

You will probably have made extensive enquiries of the seller about the business, to which many reassuring replies will have been given. But the seller is trying to persuade you to buy the business; he or she is not going to go out of the way to alert you to any problems. Inevitably, if there are problem areas, he or she is likely to want to paper over the cracks, and in doing so may give you information which is either misleading or untruthful. If you proceed to purchase on the basis of incorrect information (to use a neutral term), you may have some form of redress against the seller. However, recollection of what is said can be notoriously inaccurate; moreover, you will have the problem of proving what was said, and the only thing you can rely on is the seller denying what you claim he or she said.

There is a simple solution. Make sure that important questions are raised in writing by your solicitor and that satisfactory replies are given. An experienced solicitor should know the general queries which need to be raised, but it is for you to make sure that he or she also raises the points of particular concern to you, to cover areas such as:

- employees of the business (you need a lot of information about them in order to establish what redundancy and other rights they have)
- items on lease hire or hire-purchase: the seller cannot sell you items which do not legally belong to him or her, but you may want to take over agreements
- any work carried out or changes of use for which planning permission would have been required
- compliance with fire precautions and other safety legislation
- the identity of the landlord (if the premises are leasehold) and method of paying rent, and whether there are or have been any disputes with the landlord
- what continuing contracts can be taken over by a purchaser
- protection of goodwill.

Is there more to it?

All these enquiries will not necessarily answer the most important question: will the business be a success for you? You will need to investigate further. It helps if you can find out exactly why the business is being sold. The reason may be harmless, but there is a chance that the seller knows that the business is under some sort of threat, and is getting out while the going is good. Standard answers from sellers include retirement, poor health, moving out of the area or to a different type of business.

You will be taking over pending contracts, so check whether the seller has performed them satisfactorily so far, and whether you will be able to complete them properly, and on time.

If the business is a disaster for the seller, you will not be told directly that this is the case. But it may be revealed by the accounts.

Having satisfied yourself (so far as possible) that the business is viable, you should then try to analyse what makes it tick and to identify its strengths and any potential areas of weakness. Some businesses are heavily dependent on the personality of their owners and the departure of a popular owner from behind the counter may be followed by a decline in trade. Ask yourself also whether particular employees are vital to the image and success of the business. Some employees may be inclined to resign on the departure of a long-known boss, so you will have to win and make sure of the loyalty of any employees you regard as essential.

Last, but by no means least, take a long hard look at yourself. If the purchase proceeds, you will be one of the most important ingredients of the business. What makes you so special? (Answer this question honestly.)

The purchase – what is involved?

If the purchase of a business does not involve business premises, the transaction can be a very straightforward one. Nevertheless, you may be safer employing a solicitor. The most damaging thing that could happen is that the seller, having taken your money, immediately starts up in competition with you and wins back his or her old customers. Steps can be taken to protect you before the purchase is completed by ensuring that the seller enters into a non-competition covenant. Ask the solicitor to obtain the necessary covenant from the seller.

The majority of business purchases involve the purchase of business premises, freehold or leasehold. The position with regard to planning permission for the business must be thoroughly checked, as well as compliance with other relevant legislation. In addition, your solicitor should check whether there are any covenants adversely affecting the property or your ability to carry on a particular type of business from the premises, or whether the landlord's permission (in addition to planning permission) is required under the covenants for building work or change of use.

It is possible that with freehold covenants which were originally imposed many years ago, there is nobody legally entitled to enforce them; on the other hand, there could well be someone waiting to pounce if there is any infringement. It is possible to take out insurance for possible legal action for breach of covenants where investigation suggests that they are unenforceable.

There is a major difference between freehold and leasehold covenants. With the latter, there is inevitably someone – the landlord – who will check that they are being complied with and who will be able to take effective action if they are not.

Many business premises are leasehold (see Chapter 5), and certainly the great majority of premises found in high streets and shopping centres are so. The simple reason is cost: freehold premises are financially beyond the reach of many people who are already in business and generally all the more so of people starting their own business or seeking to buy someone else's.

The purchase contract

The contract is a document which lays down the ground rules of the purchase. Before exchange of contracts between buyer and seller, either party is at liberty to withdraw from the transaction without being liable to reimburse the other's financial outlays. After exchange of contracts, both parties are legally committed to the transaction. Any attempt by either one to withdraw risks becoming a costly experience. In any event, avoid signing any document other than the contract (and any related legal documents) provided by your solicitor.

The contract usually stipulates how the purchase price is to be split between:

- the premises
- the business goodwill
- any business equipment being sold.

Make sure you take your accountant's advice on this, because it will almost certainly have important implications for both your income tax on starting in business and for your capital gains position if/when you eventually sell.

The contract will state what business stock (also known as stock in trade) is to be sold and on what basis it is to be valued. Valuations are carried out by buyer and seller, or by a professional stock valuer. The basis of valuation should be wholesale value, often determined by reference to its purchase price. Whether or not you are likely to have any use for all the stock once you are running the business, you must expect to have to buy it all. Its value cannot be accurately assessed until it is valued at completion, so make sure that you will have sufficient funds available even if the figure turns out to be a high one. You may be able to persuade the seller to guarantee that the stock will not exceed a certain level, but be careful – if you do not have sufficient stock when you start trading, you will at once be in difficulty.

The contract will also define the trade fittings and equipment sold with the business, often in a 'schedule annexed' (that just means a list). Check that the equipment is well maintained, in good order, with an acceptable working life before it. Some items will not actually belong to the seller. Business vehicles and cash registers are generally subject to hire-purchase agreements; display freezers are sometimes lent to shop owners; burglar alarm and telephone equipment is often leased on medium- to long-term contracts. The legal position with regard to such items will need to be clarified so that (where appropriate) any agreement with their owners can be transferred into the buyer's name (yours).

If you will need any form of licence (to sell alcohol, for example) or other special permission or approval to enable you to take over the business (for example, a rest home or nursing home), the contract may need to provide that the transaction will not be completed without it.

Goodwill and its protection

Goodwill is another important issue which should be dealt with in the contract. You are buying someone else's business but what essential elements of the business can be taken over, and how can you protect yourself against the seller taking your money and then setting up in competition?

It often happens that the name under which the seller trades is included in the sale. This provides a strong appearance of continuity, and will be important if you are taking over a flourishing business, but of no value if you intend to change the name (and thus probably the image) of the business. Some trading names warrant the registration of a service mark (see Chapter 11). But not all names are the seller's to sell. For example, to trade as a Unipart Car Care Centre, a buyer will have to be approved by Unipart (this is a limited form of franchising).

Any existing custom of the business should also be included in the definition of goodwill. However, it will be entirely up to the customers whether they wish to continue to patronise the business. But a buyer would be wise to obtain a covenant from the seller which prohibits the seller from soliciting the customers of the business, and perhaps also prohibits him or her from involvement in any competing business within a defined area for a defined period.

The precise terms in which such a covenant is phrased will depend on the type and location of the business that is being sold. With many businesses, the first few weeks or months of trading are going to determine the extent of customer loyalty, and a lengthy ban on competition from the seller will not be necessary.

After exchange of contracts

It may be prudent to check all the items of trade fittings and equipment against the schedule immediately before completion. You will also need to finalise arrangements with the seller for stocktaking – ensure that this is done after he or she has stopped trading and before you start doing so.

The format of the business

If the seller runs the business in the form of a limited company, he or she will have taken advice on the best way to sell it, and you may find that he or she wants to sell it in the same form: not as just a business, but as a company. He or she does that by selling all the issued shares in exchange for a single lump sum: you then become owner of the company, and have yourself appointed director in his or her place.

You may think that this is no different from buying a business in the form of a sole trader: but there is a difference, and it is not to your advantage. When you buy a business in the form of a sole trader, it then has a new and different owner (you), and any problems from past years – for example with regard to taxation or money claims – will still be the seller's problems. You will probably be able to ignore them unless you choose to settle them, in order to enhance the business's goodwill and reputation.

But if you buy the business as a company, it still has the same owner – the company – and you inherit all past and many prospective problems, which could involve you in considerable expenditure of time and money, and prevent you from starting with a clean slate.

That is why the apparently simple matter of transferring shares is, in practice, supported by a long complicated contract which contains, among other items, a great many warranties and indemnities in favour of the buyer. But if the seller is later found to no longer have any money, these will not be worth anything.

It is wiser, therefore, to insist on buying the business without buying the company. This can be done in the name of your own company (if that is how you want to trade), and the seller should retain the original company.

If he or she refuses, you will have to decide whether to take the risk, or let the deal fall through.

Becoming a shareholder

The sale of shares in a limited company is a method frequently employed in order to raise finance, but its effect is of course to transfer part of the ownership of the company and (normally) a corresponding degree of control over it to the new owner, be they investor or otherwise.

If the owner of a limited company wants to take in a 'partner', he or she will do so by selling a portion of his or her shareholding. Care should be exercised if you are considering taking this route. The previous owner's continuing involvement (financial and managerial) in the business will, with luck, help to safeguard the prosperity of the company but you need to be certain that your business ideas agree.

If one of several shareholders in a private company is seeking to sell his or her shareholding, bear in mind that the approval of the sale by the company directors may be crucial – since they are likely to have the right to veto any sale by the simple expedient of refusing to register a transfer of shares.

The value of a company is relatively easy to determine, although there are differing accounting conventions for doing so. But the value of a partial shareholding, particularly a minority shareholding, in the same company can be very difficult both to assess and to realise. The most important variable factor will be any restrictions that may exist on the owner's ability to sell. If the other shareholders are the only available market, you may have either to accede to their price or else to hang on to your shares – a dilemma that arises all too frequently.

These problems can be circumvented by agreement between the shareholders, but it is important that you take sound legal advice before committing yourself.

Becoming a partner

Becoming a partner in an existing business is very different from becoming a member (shareholder) in an existing limited company. Your legal liabilities to the outside world only start from the moment you become a partner; by contrast, in purchasing a company's shares you are buying the company's on-going obligations as well as its assets. And while buying shares necessarily implies a stake in all the company's assets, entering into a partnership does not automatically mean that you will acquire any rights of ownership over the partnership assets.

You need to understand too that if you enter into an unlimited partnership you are 'jointly and severally' liable for any debts of the partnership (with the exception of tax, see 'Partnership' at the beginning of this chapter). In other words you are liable for your partner's share of debts, as well as your own. You should ensure (as far as you are able) that prospective partners are trustworthy and that they have sufficient assets to cover their likely share of any debts.

It is important to enter into a written agreement with the existing partners covering at least such essential issues as profit sharing and ownership of the firm's assets. These issues may at first seem clear-cut, but on reflection you will find that they are not. In the long run, ambiguity and uncertainty, if unresolved, only lead to unnecessary conflict.

Chapter 4

Marketing and selling

Marketing and selling your product or service are not just incidental to producing it: they are the lifeblood of the business.

The two terms are not interchangeable. Marketing covers everything from research, product planning and development to promotion and, of course, selling. Selling is the process of negotiating and carrying out that transaction.

Emerson was mistaken: the world will not beat a path to your house to clamour for your better mousetrap. However efficient it may be, if you do not go to town and seek out people with mice, it will be left on your hands.

In fact, before you started to design it, you should have checked on the mouse population, and the cat population too; it never does to ignore one's competitors.

What is more, when you have found your customers, and are busy with orders, you must plan for future sales. Selling is a continuous process: you should always be looking ahead and planning your marketing strategy for the coming months and years.

The time to start planning for sales is when your product or service is still on the drawing-board. At this point, nothing is lost if you discover that your idea, however good of its kind, will not command a large enough market to make a profit. Perhaps it will be so expensive to produce that its price will be prohibitive; or, perhaps, there are not enough people who long for, say, reproduction antique musical boxes. You still have a chance to rethink it and eliminate expensive labour-intensive processes, for example; or modify it to give it more popular appeal; or scrap it altogether in favour of something else. Begin by asking yourself some questions:

- What exactly have I got to offer my customers?
- Who are likely to be my customers, and where shall I find them?
- Who are my competitors, and in what way is my product an improvement on theirs or a better alternative (mousetrap v. poison)?
- What is the best way of making my product or service known to the customer?
- When do I start planning for the future?

What exactly have I got to offer?

Defining just what it is that you are going to put on the market cannot be done in isolation. You will also have to consider to whom, how, when and where you are going to sell.

Consider your product

If what you are going to sell is something produced by other people, for which you are going to act as retailer or middleman, agent or dealer, you probably have no influence on the actual form of the product. The choice is between one brand and another, between the cheap and popular or the expensive and exclusive varieties of the product.

However, if it is something you have produced or designed (or had designed for you) and intend to produce, you can decide what the final form of the product will be. You can decide to produce it in several versions, with varying functions, and at different price levels; you may make it highly specialised, with only one use, or you may incorporate several functions, in order to widen its appeal; or make it part of a range of related products; or change the materials of which it is made; or scrap it altogether and start again. Do not fall in love with the original idea and insist on going through with it, come hell or high water.

It may be unwise to include every possible refinement right from the start; a highly specialised product may appeal only to a small market. A simpler version may sell better and also pave the way for a more complex one, to be developed now and introduced at a later stage, incorporating new features in response to what were the first customers' reactions.

If your product is more sophisticated than the prospective buyers are likely to demand, or too expensive for the ultimate consumer, you must simplify the product or decide to find another market for it, or produce two varieties for different types of user.

If the product requires the skills of several craftspeople, for example cabinet-maker and precision engineer, make sure from the start that you will have a supply of skilled labour to depend on. It is no use building up a market for a product if you cannot maintain the supply. It might be better to design something that can be made by less skilled labour.

Ask yourself if the demand for your product is likely to be seasonal. A new nutcracker, for example, however super-efficient, is likely to sell readily only in the period before Christmas, so you may need another product (or several) to keep your plant and labour occupied for the rest of the year.

Where what you have to sell is quite simply a service plus your expertise, the need to define it precisely applies just as much as to a product. If, for example, you are setting up a security business, you should decide whether you are best able to supply a delivery service (complete with armoured cars), or human guards, or guard dogs, or specialist advice on how people can improve the security of their home or factory.

In the case of a consultancy or agency, too, define your scope as closely as possible, and relate it to your own experience. Rather than grandly planning to become an import-export agent, aim to trade with particular geographical areas and in specific products, preferably areas and products with which you are already familiar. When setting up as a consultant, you are more likely to succeed if you closely limit your field to where your particular expertise lies. Do not wait for your clients' reactions to tell you on what topics you are not qualified to give advice.

Who are my customers and where shall I find them?

The nature of the product or service will dictate a general answer: woollen sweaters are for people, automated filing systems are for offices, easy-to-install damp-proof window frames should interest the building industry and the d-i-y enthusiast. A solar-panel water heating system may currently have a limited market in Britain, but could be the basis of an export trade until the domestic market develops.

Next, get some idea of how you should sell your products to your prospective customers, whether through a retail shop or a department store, through a wholesaler or by mail order, through agents or directly, in the UK or abroad.

Some market research

Researching your market is not as formidable as it sounds. You can do a lot of 'market research' yourself from sources ready to hand, starting with public libraries.

The central library in your area should have a comprehensive reference department. In the commercial section you will find trade directories and publications relating to your business; the *Yellow Pages* and phone books covering the whole country; directories of foreign importers; official digests of statistics, and much more.

In London, you can command the superb resources of the City Business Library or Westminster Reference Library, but the chief town or city in your area should offer facilities.

The Government Statistical Services make available, on demand, a vast amount of information gathered by the Office for National Statistics (ONS)★ and by government departments. The booklet *Government Statistics: A Brief Guide to Sources*, available free from the ONS, lists the various kinds of facts and figures available, including aspects of business, such as industrial production, financial services, the retail trade and external trade. Much of this is published in a series called *Business Monitors*.

Someone planning a comprehensive marketing strategy may want to study figures relating to national income and expenditure and population trends and projections. This may sound grandiose but what it amounts to is that you might get an idea of what proportion of what kind of people (teenagers, pensioners, etc.) is likely to want your product.

Some publications for useful facts and figures include: *UK Directory of Manufacturing Businesses*; *UK Markets* (125 separate reports); *Population Trends* (quarterly); *Family Spending* (annual); *Overseas Trade Statistics of the United Kingdom* (monthly); and *UK Service Sector: Retail Sales* (monthly). Ask for them at the public library as they are rather expensive. Useful free publications are also available from your local Business Link* or alternative centre (see Chapter 1).

Trade organisations, trade journals, trade exhibitions

As a novice, you should snatch at every opportunity of consulting those who are already experts: your own trade organisation should be able to help you. Trade associations are listed in the *Directory of British Associations* (available in reference libraries). Journals and exhibitions will inform you about the prospects of your trade, future developments and new products, and will give you an idea of who your potential buyers might be. The *Financial Times* publishes the dates and venues of forthcoming trade exhibitions. So, too, does the *Exhibition Bulletin*.* The information it offers is worldwide in scope and two years or more in advance, which makes planning ahead easier.

If your product is to be sold to some trade or industry, you can use its trade directories to compile a list of potential customers.

You may find details of some more relevant journals and publications by looking at *Brads Media Lists* which are categorised by subject.

Wherever economics or business studies are taught – at universities, local technical colleges, schools of business studies – you should be able to find a library, experts to consult, even students willing, for a modest fee, to do your market research for you. Make the arrangement, preferably in the autumn term, through the Management Studies or Trading Department.

Dry run

If you have started to manufacture your product in your spare time and are wondering whether to go into full production, try to test your market. This can be done for a small outlay, perhaps by distributing a few hundred leaflets, or putting a couple of dozen cards in shop windows. Do not distribute too many leaflets at a time, in case you would then not be able to deal with the number of requests. Space out the distribution. This should give you some idea of whether anyone in the district is interested in what you have to offer.

Who are my competitors?

The *Yellow Pages* will tell you what other similar businesses there are in your area, if you are counting on local trade.

Make yourself familiar with your competitors' products. Watch particularly for competitors' publicity and advertising: yours will have to be different and better. Send for their promotional literature and price lists. You should also attend trade exhibitions. Trade directories and the trade press will give you relevant addresses.

If yours is a service industry, try approaching a similar firm for advice. You may find one operating in another area that is remarkably willing to show you round the premises and answer questions. But do not expect your local firms to welcome and train more competition, and do not, in your enthusiasm, give your ideas away to someone who may beat you to it.

If the competitor's product is sold through retail outlets, go and see it at the point of sale to find out how it is displayed and promoted.

The object is to find out how your product would compare. Has it any unique features? Why should people prefer it to any other? What special features have the other products got that could be incorporated in your product (with due regard to infringement of copyright or patents)? Something as simple as a hook, a lid, a heatproof base, could make all the difference to the appeal of a gadget.

How do I sell my products?

The actual business of putting anything on the market has several aspects including advertising, sales and distribution, and pricing.

Advertising and promotion

Which of the various media you should use will depend very much on the nature of your product (or service), and how much you can afford to spend on making it known.

The local press is particularly suited to a service or business which relies on local customers, such as a plumber, electrician, hairdresser, launderette, florist. The cheapest advertisement is an insert in the classified advertisement section. This kind of advertisement does not catch the eye: it simply waits for someone looking for that type of service or product. So, to be effective, it should appear regularly. If you want to catch the reader's passing glance, a display advertisement will be more effective or, if your budget permits, a larger, specially designed advertisement, placed on an editorial page (perhaps with a 'Freepost' coupon on which further information can be requested – see 'Making the most of the post' – but then the return postage must be budgeted for). Such an advertisement, too, should appear regularly. A coupon is most effective when placed on the outside edge of the page, where it is easy to cut out.

Many local papers will design a display advertisement but a professionally designed one is likely to be more eyecatching. You can find a graphic designer through the *Yellow Pages*, but before commissioning him or her, make sure you know the cost.

Advertising in national newspapers and magazines is suited to a firm hoping to sell by mail order. It is essential to choose publications that are right for the type of goods – women's clothing in women's pages and magazines, sets of spanners in d-i-y magazines.

The trade press is the medium for goods that are sold not to individual consumers but to other firms. Much the same considerations apply as in the case of the national press; and where your advertisement is likely to appear cheek-by-jowl with those of competitors, it is essential to have an effective display that stands out. There are plenty of small local advertising agencies whose names can be found in the *Yellow Pages,* or the Institute of Practitioners in Advertising (IPA)* can supply them. Ask to see specimens of work and get an estimate before you engage one.

What you will be paying for is know-how. An agency should be able to design your advertising, advise on its content and wording, and place it in the appropriate media at the right times.

Trade exhibitions and local trade fairs have a triple function – for market research, for finding out what your competitors are producing, and also for selling your own goods to firms. They are not usually open to the general public. Your trade press will tell you where and when appropriate exhibitions are taking place, and where to apply to book space. There may be several suitable ones each year.

Exhibitions can be expensive; as well as hiring the stand, you must arrange for someone competent to be there to run it, explain and perhaps demonstrate your product, distribute literature and note down enquiries (to be scrupulously followed up). Probably that person will have to be you, with consequent loss of your valuable time. The exhibition should at least earn back its expenses eventually, so do not rush in too readily without thought and preparation.

You are more likely to attract the buyers' attention if you write to them beforehand, preferably by name (which you can find out by telephoning their firms). Send them your promotional literature and the number of your stand, and invite them to have a chat with you.

If you cannot afford a stand, or if your range of goods does not rate one, ask the Chamber of Commerce or your Small Business Club for the names of any other firms who might be willing to share a stand. Or you may be able to find out from the promoters of the exhibition the names of firms which are exhibiting related products. Approach them to ask if they will lease you a share of their space and attendants.

Direct mail advertising

With direct mail advertising, you approach the customer directly, and by name. You send out a sales letter, accompanied by a leaflet, brochure or catalogue. The promotional literature should be eye-catching, and designed by a professional, if possible.

Making the most of the post

Business Reply and Freepost are two of the services offered by Royal Mail to direct mail advertisers. With Business Reply, you send out, for your customer's reply, a postcard or envelope printed with your address and needing no stamp: first and second class options are available. With Freepost, the customer can use either pre-printed cards or envelopes provided by you (first or second class), or use his or her own stationery (second class only). No stamp is needed if the word 'Freepost' is added to the address.

You pay only the postage, first or second class as you wish, plus (with the standard service) a small handling charge on each reply you receive, in addition to an annual licence fee.

If you want to direct your advertising to one or more whole areas, rather than to specific addresses, you should find the Door to Door service useful. This arranges for your advertising to be delivered by the regular postmen on their rounds. The charge for this to you is based on the weight of the material: there are five weight categories, with a 100g maximum. The more you send, the lower the rates (but there is a £500 minimum charge).

Royal Mail also offers Mailsort, a range of discount services for presorted mail which apply to bulk mailings of 4,000 or more letters or 1,000 or more packets, provided these have been sorted in advance by the sender, according to postcode. Bear in mind that you will have to pay someone to do the sorting, so these services are unlikely to prove useful until your business has expanded greatly.

Further details of these and other services can be obtained from Royal Mail Sales Centres.★ Royal Mail also offers advice on creating effective mailshots through its *Complete Guide to Advertising Your Business by Post*, also available from its Sales Centres.

Mailing lists

You do not, of course, write to the population at large; you need a mailing list of people likely to be interested. If you want to sell to an industry or trade, you can make up your own mailing list out of entries in the trade directories; this is laborious but relatively inexpensive.

It is more effective if you can find out the name of each firm's buyer – from a trade reference book, the appropriate trade association or by telephoning the firm – and address the letter individually to him or her, making it appear unique. A good word-processing computer package should be able to handle this.

If your customer information is kept on computer files, then it is subject to the Data Protection Act 1984, which is concerned with regulating the use of information about living individuals that is held on computer (known as personal data). The Act places obligations upon those that hold and use personal data (known as data users). Data users must be open about that use by registering under the Act, and they are bound by the eight Data Protection Principles contained within it. Full details can be obtained from the Office of the Data Protection Registrar.★ Note that under a new Data Protection Bill due be introduced some time in 1998, some manual (i.e. non-computerised) records will also be covered by the legislation.

For advertising to local firms, relevant names and addresses from the *Yellow Pages* can be used in the same way.

For advertising to individual consumers, you can try to make up your own mailing list from the electoral register.

Many organisations have subscription or membership lists that they may be willing to rent out to you, for a fee. If the list is very large, they may agree to let you have part of it, even just a very small part, so that you can test how well the list works for your purposes. Do not be too surprised, however, if the part that you are offered for the test turns out to be the best part of the list. To get a more realistic idea of how useful the list is going to be to you, ask for a cross-section – say, one out of every six names. A large percentage of any full list is likely to be postally undeliverable – 'no such address' or 'gone away'.

You may be able to buy the list, in which case you will receive the names and addresses and can use them as often as you like, for whatever purpose you like. However, very few organisations sell their lists; they rather rent them out or exchange lists. Exchanging means that two organisations use each others' lists – but you, as a beginner, will not have anything to swap.

The organisation may make it a condition to have sight of and approve the offer which is to be mailed. To prevent you from copying their lists, they may insist that the addressing and posting are done by a specialist mailing company.

You will, of course, learn the names and addresses of those who reply, and they then become part of your own list, which you later may sell, rent out or exchange. There are a number of list brokers who may be able to help you find lists, for a fee. Look for list brokers who are members of the Direct Marketing Association,★ as these should meet certain standards concerning how, for example, the list is compiled.

Counting the cost

First calculate the likely cost, and be clear how to assess the responses; 26p per name and address may not sound much, but if the response rate is 1 per cent, the cost becomes £26 per reply.

The response rate to direct mail advertising is variable, depending on the product, the market and the care taken in preparation: a response of between 3 and 5 per cent should be considered as extremely good. Naturally, not every enquiry results in an order; after your first mailshot you should be able to calculate whether the resulting business has earned back its promotion costs plus some profit.

Leaflet distribution is a humbler, localised version of direct mail. At its simplest, this could be a leaflet pushed through a few hundred neighbourhood doors. You may be able to arrange for a newsagent to slip a leaflet inside every newspaper delivered, for a fee.

If you want to cover larger or more distant areas, you will have to entrust the work to a specialist firm: look in the *Yellow Pages* under 'Addressing/Circularising Services', and 'Circular/Sample

Distributors'. Thomson Directories publishes a booklet to help the advertising novice. The *Advertising Handbook* gives useful advice on planning every kind of advertising campaign, and includes a summary of all the main advertising media. It is free from the Customer Care Department of Thomson Directories.★

Mailing Preference Service

The use of direct mail is a very effective form of advertising, but it needs to be used with particular care. Many members of the public resent receiving mail addressed to them by name from a company with which they have had no contact and of which they may not have heard. They are then very likely simply to throw away what they consider to be 'junk mail', without a second glance. It is therefore in the advertiser's interest to subscribe to the Mailing Preference Service.★

The MPS makes available to subscribers a quarterly listing of people who have positively requested that they should not be sent any direct mail advertising. It also makes available a list of those people who have asked to be sent more details of goods available in some particular category. If you do your mailing through a list broker or a mailing house, make sure that it uses an 'MPS-cleaned' list.

Press releases

Any event of special interest in your firm, such as the opening of a new workshop or the launching of a new product, should be communicated to the local and trade press in the form of a press release. Do not be intimidated by the term 'press release' – all you have to do is find out who is in charge of, say, the technical page of the newspaper and then write to them with a suitable small article. Make sure that the relevant details – the name of the product, your name, your address, and the prices are included. The better written and more concise the article, the more likely it is to get in. Pictures help, but they should be black and white. If what you send catches editorial attention, and secures a paragraph or two of editorial copy, this is often more effective than any advertisement. If you place an advertisement at the same time, you may get an editorial mention – but the two are not invariably linked.

To get mentioned in the national press is helpful for anyone selling by mail order. Try to think of people who would be interested in your story, for example the women's page editor.

Selling

You will need to consider the question of distribution and selling long before you can manufacture enough to satisfy widespread demand.

Selling to shops

At the most basic level, this is a question of taking round a sample of your product to appropriate shops in the district and persuading them to stock it. To go about this sensibly, you need to:

- Make an appointment to see the shop's owner or manager; do not simply turn up unannounced at the busiest time.
- Make yourself familiar with competing products, their prices and their drawbacks, so that you can point out the advantages of yours (without obvious criticism of rival products).
- Be clear about the price of your product, but be willing to allow the retailer an attractive discount. The real problem is to decide whether or not to sell on sale or return. On the whole, it is better not to, but if you find that one particular line does not move and others do, you could offer to buy it back in order to get the shop to take more of the merchandise that does sell.
- Be prepared to prove that you can guarantee supplies and will stick to delivery dates.
- Have the product or range of your products properly packaged, as it will look when displayed in a shop window or on a shelf.
- Sometimes it also helps to offer a small display aid, to show your product to its best advantage. Make clear to the shop owner that this is on loan to display your product, not a gift, nor for use to show off someone else's goods.

The technique for larger shops, or chain stores, is to start by contacting the appropriate buyer in each store. The retail directory (from a reference library) gives some names; find out others by telephoning. Make an appointment to see each buyer:

- Pay particular attention to the presentation of your product.
- Know your maximum capacity and the size of orders you can guarantee to deliver and your most dependable delivery dates.
- Be prepared to prove that you can finance your increased output.

- When you come to discuss the price, be sure to have some room for negotiating. But remember, some large shops will expect extended credit terms and will delay payment.

Most large companies pay on a 30-day account: that is, they pay invoices on their first accounting day occurring when 30 days have passed from receipt of the invoice. (It is important to invoice customers promptly and correctly, offering no excuse for further delaying payment.)

If you negotiate a major contract, ask for stage payments: for instance, part payment with the order and then percentage payments at various stages of production or delivery. For more on getting paid see Chapter 13.

Pricing

The price you charge for a product or service can be arrived at in various ways. Economists have theories about price based on costs, based on competition, based on the demand, based on the going rate; in real life for a small business, these categories tend to slide into each other.

Pricing based on costs is a crude but still commonly used method. The price is made up of the cost of the product to the manufacturer (labour, materials, overheads) plus a percentage mark-up to give what you consider to be a fair profit. Your own costs will set the lower limit. This method, however, ignores two important factors: demand and competition. Unless you are selling bread during a famine, demand will set an upper limit on what you can charge, and so will the presence in the market of competitors.

You must allow for discounts for quantity orders, or for payment in seven days and for anything else that might encourage greater purchase or quicker settlement.

If you sell to the final consumer, by retail or through mail order, there is no problem with getting payment; but if you sell to another firm, you will need to offer credit – because the competition does and you must cost that in.

If you sell through a wholesaler your price must allow for the wholesaler's and retailer's profit as well as your own. The price to the customer will contain the three elements of the wholesaler's mark-up, the retailer's mark-up and your profit (plus VAT if applicable). You must allow for these in order not to price yourself out of the market.

Pricing based on competition

It is important to identify your competitors and to make yourself familiar with what they are offering at what prices. You can, to a large extent, be guided by what competitors are asking for a comparable product.

For most products there are several price ranges, and manufacturers deliberately tailor their goods to fit into one of these. Some manufacturers produce several product ranges, each one for a different category. Cosmetics, for instance, tend to be cheap and cheerful for the young, medium priced for the average user, and extremely expensive for the wealthier consumer. You should decide at an early stage into which price category your product will slot.

If you cannot fit into the lower or middle range, because your costs are high, you will have to aim at the higher category; but then you will have to make sure that the prices reflect some special and unique quality of your goods, and show the customer that this is so. There are some categories of goods – cosmetics, again, are an example – where a high price can actually be a selling point: the customer is reassured that it is a unique, luxury article, and it would be an error of psychology to charge less.

Another way of taking demand into account is this. If you produce a range of related goods, some will be more in demand than others; your pricing should therefore be based on a profit margin averaged out over the whole range.

Or you may try loss-leader pricing of one or more items, at cost, or very little above it, as a bait to capture a large share of the market quickly. But you will be the loser if you sell all the low-profit items and none of the high-profit ones.

Pricing based on the going rate incorporates the elements of competition and of demand. It is the way of pricing in most service industries. Where there is no going rate, you must cost your own time very carefully when calculating your overheads. But, usually, there is a recognised going rate for the service, and in order to charge more you would need to offer something that was out of the ordinary, such as being on call at all hours, or offering a particularly comprehensive service.

Face-to-face selling

Many people who would find no difficulty in selling goods across a shop counter feel deeply embarrassed when it comes to calling on firms to offer their goods or services.

Aggressive selling is, however, rarely required: one's best weapon is a detailed knowledge of one's project and a readiness to explain it fluently, and even demonstrate it.

Present as good an appearance as possible: as a small entrepreneur you will inspire more confidence by a show of frugal efficiency than by lavish trimmings. (For some kinds of service, such as consultancy perhaps, appearances are very important, since you may have nothing else to show your client.)

Keep good records of your customers, how much they buy and when – a computer could prove useful. Keep in constant touch, so that when they think of buying, you are in the forefront of their minds. Ask them if they are satisfied, and treat complaints in a friendly spirit; look into the complaint and put right anything that needs rectifying. Genuinely listen to what the potential customer says, and show an obvious interest in what he or she wants.

In many cases you must be able to offer a service, as well as a product: installation, spare parts and servicing. Make sure that you have the facilities for this, or next time the customer may go elsewhere. If you cannot provide the service yourself, find a sub-contractor.

Know your potential customer's own products and be able to discuss them intelligently, and if you personally happen to use a competitor's product, keep this to yourself.

Employing an agent

If you dislike or have no talent for selling, or do not have time for it, you may be better occupied concentrating on the production side, while getting someone else to sell for you. You might think of persuading a golden-tongued friend to do you the favour, if only for the initial contacting, but a proper business partner, or, best of all for this purpose, a proper agent, is preferable.

The advantages for a new business can be considerable. An agent will have the necessary contacts, and be known in the trade; he or she can also keep you informed about what your competitors are doing. Your agent will need to be primed with any necessary technical information and supplied with promotional literature, possibly backed up with advertising.

The disadvantage is that the agent's commission reduces your profit margin – but perhaps you would not have had the profit at all, but for him or her.

An agent usually represents more than one firm, and you can never guarantee that the agent is trying as hard for you as for the others: he or she naturally works hardest for products offering the highest return.

To find an agent, consult one or all of the following: the trade press; trade directories; *Yellow Pages* (under 'Manufacturers' Agents' and 'Marketing/Advertising Consultants'); or advertise for one yourself. You can negotiate any agreement that seems suitable, but both parties must be quite clear about the terms before starting.

Mail order selling

Direct response mail order selling is a system in which press advertisements urge customers to order goods, which are then sent to them directly.

Payment is usually by cash (cheque) with order or by credit card; it is usual to offer free approval ('money back if not delighted') which is required by most of the relevant codes of practice. Some firms offer credit terms, but these are usually catalogue mail order houses rather than firms selling their own products.

To be suitable for mail order selling, the product should fall into one or more of the following categories:

* light in weight and strong enough not to break in transit, or bulky but capable of being compactly and securely packed (for example, many types of garden sheds and greenhouses are sold by mail order)
* aimed at a market where the convenience of buying by post or telephone outweighs the disadvantage of not being able to see the product before the purchase

- not obtainable in ordinary retail shops, that is, in some way new, unique or hard to find – for example a craft product, or something for a minority taste, or obtainable in shops, but at a much higher price. Make sure, however, that the customer's postage costs do not take away your price advantage. Because of postage, very low-priced articles are not worth selling by mail.

Your customers must be left in no doubt about the total cost of any goods offered. In particular, make clear whether the costs of packing and postage or delivery are included in the price, and if not, what these costs are.

Not only your production but your packing, despatch and administration must be up to scratch. Before starting the operation be sure that you have the stocks and the extra capacity to meet a sudden increase in demand, and are able to deliver goods within the promised period. This should be within 30 days. If you suddenly find that an order cannot be sent off within the period you promised, you should immediately contact the buyer and offer a refund; or if the customer chooses to wait, he or she should be given a firm date for the despatch of the order or fortnightly progress reports.

These points, and very many others with which you must comply in this form of selling, are contained in the code of practice of the Direct Marketing Association (UK) Ltd.★ The DMA code is binding only on members of the Association.

You must conform to both the legal requirements and the voluntary codes of practice governing mail order selling. And to advertise in the national press you should get clearance from the National Newspapers' Mail Order Protection Scheme Ltd,★ which runs a Mail Order Protection Scheme (MOPS). You must pay a fee to a central fund which indemnifies readers against loss due to a firm's failure to supply goods ordered if it is liquidated or ceases to trade. If you are approved to join, you must display the MOPS logo in your advertisement.

Similar schemes are operated by many local papers. To advertise in magazines you will need to comply with the conditions of the Mail Order Protection Scheme as operated by members of the Periodical Publishers Association★. Unlike the National Press Association MOPS, the PPA scheme is not centrally run, nor funded by contributions from advertisers. Instead, each individual publisher requires would-be advertisers to complete application forms asking for details of their business. On the basis of this information, a judgment is made as to whether the applicants should be allowed to solicit money off the page in the publications. Further details of the PPA scheme can be obtained from the Periodical Publishers Association.

There are some exemptions from MOPS, such as perishable goods. Whether or not your product is exempt, it must conform to the British Codes of Advertising and Sales Promotion. To ensure that your advertisement will be acceptable, contact the Advertising Standards Authority:* its Copy Advice Team will give you (confidential) advice and discuss your proposals with you.

Make sure that you have an efficient system (perhaps on computer) for recording the product sold, the dates of purchase and despatch, and the name and address of each customer (which are then added to your own mailing list). Note, however, that if you process personal data of this type you must register the uses, classes, sources and disclosures of this data with the Data Protection Registrar and comply with the eight Data Protection Principles. It is a criminal offence to collect or use personal data without having registered. In addition, industry guidelines on direct marketing, including list and database practice, are contained within the British Codes of Advertising and Sales Promotion, available from the Advertising Standards Authority.

As with direct mail advertising, ask the postal services representative about reduced terms for bulk parcel despatch.

If you advertise in several newspapers and magazines, it is worth using a simple code to distinguish replies from each source, so that you can tell which one brings in the most business.

The price you charge for your product must take into account the advertising costs – often as much as one third of the selling price – as well as the cost of replacing damaged articles, and, if you offer credit, of bad debts. If you sell on credit, or free approval, allow for this in your cash flow forecasting.

Providing credit card facilities may be worthwhile, since it allows the customer to obtain credit without risk to yourself – your money is guaranteed, provided you adhere to the conditions.

If you are interested in accepting cards, telephone the local card area sales office (the bank's local enquiries line or business banking centre should be able to give you the number) to obtain details. If necessary, they will arrange for a representative to call to discuss the arrangements. There is a service charge or commission of up to 5 per cent, which depends on the size of the business, plus, in most cases, an initial fee of, say, £100, so you will have to build these costs into your pricing or wait until your business is big enough to bring the costs down.

Using the phone

If selling over the phone brings images of double glazing to mind, think again: 'telemarketing', as it is known, is a growth area and has a broad range of uses. In particular, telemarketing can be used to back up a sales promotion or advertising campaign, leaving you free to concentrate on the product. For example, a telemarketing bureau could send out product details, handle questions about what you have to offer or even take orders.

Telephone services are also increasingly used as a way of giving 'after-sales' customer care. If failing to offer such a service would put your business at a competitive disadvantage, you need to take this into account from the start, either by offering some form of customer care yourself or by choosing some other ground on which to compete.

Dealing with customers by phone needs to be handled sensitively to avoid having the opposite of the desired effect. BT★ publishes two useful guides, *Talking Better Business* and *Talking Better Business Essentials*, which are available free. The Direct Marketing Association★ can provide a list of telemarketing bureaux which are members and which should therefore comply with its code of practice, or look in the *Yellow Pages* under 'Telemarketing'.

If you are considering contacting potential customers by telephone make sure that whoever you use for telemarketing is registered with the Telephone Preference Service.★ Run by the same organisation as the Mailing Preference Service, it makes available lists of people who have requested not to be contacted by telephone.

Selling in a very small way

Market stalls and country fairs provide an outlet for a small business making a slow, cautious start at selling, and are particularly suited to craft goods. The local authority will be able to tell you where and when fairs are held in the district, and who to contact about renting a stall, either permanently or by the day.

Exhibiting at a local craft fair could be a good way of launching a product. Some craft associations will arrange to exhibit members' work. The *Showman's Directory*★ will give you a list of 'non-craft' events throughout the country, which might be of use in finding appropriate locations for selling or publicity; it will also tell you where to hire marquees and other equipment.

Chapter 5

Premises

The question of premises obviously varies according to the type of business. The kind of space you need to work in will depend largely on whether you manufacture goods, or sell them, or offer a service.

Advice about the regulations

Offices, shops, factories and many other types of commercial accommodation have to comply with regulations about the safety of staff and facilities for them; so it is as well to be sure that one's prospective premises either accord with the regulations, or are capable of being converted so as to comply with them. Information about this can be obtained from the Health and Safety Executive's InfoLine* and free leaflets from its publications section, HSE Books.*

You can also get information from the planning department of your local authority.

Premises for a service industry

If you provide a service, for example as a builder, decorator or plumber, probably all of your work will be carried on in your customers' premises. To begin with you will only need some space at home in which to do the paperwork, and perhaps a shed or garage for storing tools. However, if your business thrives and grows, and you come to employ workers, you will eventually need an office to deal with enquiries, estimates and paperwork, and also larger storage space, and parking for your vans – proper business premises, in fact.

If your business is a consultancy or agency needing little or no equipment, the physical location of your office may not be crucial to your success. You may require only a room or two and find it convenient to make over some part of your house to business use.

Serviced offices

Serviced offices are available for a weekly or monthly charge, offering such things as the rent of an office full-time or just an occasional meeting room, telephone answering services, voice mail, fax services and post forwarding. A particular advantage, if you are doing business overseas, is that it is possible to get a base in other countries in this way. For names of organisations running serviced offices, look in the *Yellow Pages* under 'Office Rental'.

Serviced offices may be convenient, and depending on the location, allow you to present an up-market image, but it is vital to check the terms and conditions. How long are you committed for? What is the landlord legally committed to provide – and what comeback is there if the services supplied are not up to scratch? It is worth talking to other users of the service to see what their experience has been, and also checking whether you could put together your own package. For example, telephone answering and voice mail are available from telephone operators, fax machines are now relatively cheap to buy, and rather than commit yourself to an office you could rent conference rooms in a local hotel for meetings as and when you need them.

Working from home

Obviously, for a very small and new business there is a tremendous advantage in working from home: you save on rent, rates, cost of the public utilities, cleaning – and even staff, if a member of your family answers the door and the telephone and perhaps does the typing.

However, some house deeds prohibit use for business purposes, and many restrictive covenants of this type would be enforceable. Even where there are no such restrictions, if you carry on a business from residential premises, you may need planning permission from the local authority and may have to pay higher charges for commercial occupation. You should, in any event, inform the company that is insuring your house. Using it for business, particularly if you are storing any combustible goods, may invalidate the buildings and contents insurance – even against totally unrelated disasters, such as a burst water pipe.

There are plenty of small businesses run inconspicuously from home without permission because there is nothing in the work to inconvenience the neighbours or to alert snoopers. But if you want to be above-board in carrying on your business, or if your house needs to be altered for the purpose, as in adding a room or shed, you may need planning permission. A fee is payable when an application for planning permission is submitted to the local authority.

The permission may be qualified by some conditions relating to hours of work, or callers at the house. If your application is refused, you have the right to appeal, but if this fails, you may have no choice but to look elsewhere for accommodation.

If you claim a proportion of the expenses of running your home as a business expense, there is a risk of your having to pay capital gains tax on the same proportion of the gains realised when you eventually sell the house. A small gain may well fall within your exempt allowance for the year in which you sell, but be sure to check the position with your accountant.

Premises for a manufacturing business

Unless you are a craftsperson working single-handed and in a very small business, it is unlikely that you will be able to work from home: apart from probable lack of workshop space, you may well run into opposition from the local authority or neighbours.

A manufacturing firm has to satisfy zoning regulations for light and heavy industry, because it may create noise, smoke, fumes, industrial waste that must be disposed of, and other sorts of environmental pollution; or it may increase the risk of fire. It is extremely unlikely that you could carry on a manufacturing business clandestinely, or that you would get permission to do so in residential premises.

As for renting workshop space, even at times when there are many millions of square feet of factory premises vacant in Britain, only a small percentage of this may be suitable for a business which is just starting up. Just the same, there is no reason why you should not get hold of some of this percentage if you go about it the right way.

Hunting for workshop space

Define your exact requirements. You will need a site big enough to allow your firm to settle down and expand, because you may not want to have to move in a year or two. There must be access to all the mains services; warehousing space; room and amenities for the workers; parking space; room for lorries to load and unload. You probably do not need a central situation or a street frontage, but you must ensure that any noise, fumes, smoke etc., do not annoy people living nearby, especially during overtime working.

You may need an office if you expect customers to be calling on you. There may be a number of other requirements: it is unlikely that any one site will satisfy all of them.

Begin by contacting your local Business Link* or alternative (see Chapter 1). They will know the sorts of help that are available in your area, and where to find out more. For example, some local authorities try to cater for the very small business by building 'nursery' units, which are simply shells, sometimes only 500 square feet (about the size of a double garage). The rents are not necessarily low. But, if the authority is anxious to promote employment, it may subsidise them or offer other incentives.

Some councils keep a register of vacant industrial property, and may be able to help you by extracting from this a list of suitable properties. Most local authorities recognise that their attitude to small business can affect unemployment levels, and are as helpful as they can be.

But if official bodies cannot help, you must make the rounds of local estate agents. If you do resort to these, remember that they may need telephoning at intervals to remind them of your existence. Low-cost, low-rental premises have little value to an agent because they bring in a low fee. Very small and cheap premises in the centre of town do not always reach the estate agents' lists, so keep your eyes open, and also study the classified advertisements in the local press. Members of the local Small Business Club can be a good source of information and advice.

When you find a place that seems suitable, there are still a number of factors to be considered, for instance, whether to buy or to lease.

Buying a lease

While some business premises are sold freehold, the majority of them are only available on lease. For someone starting in business, a lease has the considerable advantage of being relatively inexpensive to acquire and of not necessarily calling for a long-term commitment.

In buying leasehold premises you will almost certainly be buying the assignment of an existing lease that was negotiated between the landlord and the original tenant. This document will regulate your legal relationship with the landlord, so read it very carefully and get your solicitor to explain the more technical aspects of it. Business leases are highly technical documents: employ a solicitor experienced in this field. Your Business Link★ may have information on specialist solicitors in your area.

A new lease is more likely to be negotiated if it is the landlord (the freeholder) who is the seller of the business. Inevitably, a landlord will seek to bias the document in his or her own favour, but there may be room for bargaining. Remember that it is worth taking the trouble to get the terms of the lease right – once it is agreed and signed, it must be assumed to be unchangeable.

A lease tends to be an intimidating document. But sit down and read it, and also the various schedules attached, and mark (in pencil and on a copy) the points which are important to you or which you do not understand. Ask for clarification and then read it again. Here is a brief guide to some of the issues with which the lease deals, and the questions you need to ask about it.

Rent

The rent will probably be payable in instalments each year. What is the current rent? When is it next due to be reviewed? Will the new rent be linked to the retail prices index (unlikely), or determined by reference to rentals of comparable premises? What other payments will be due to the landlord (for example, insurance, service charges)?

Cost of purchase

There can be a substantial difference between a new and an existing lease in terms of cost of purchase. A tenant selling a lease may ask for a 'premium' (a capital sum) to be paid by the incoming tenant, and this will be determined by market forces. For example, a lease at a low rent or for a particularly attractive retail site might attract a considerable premium, whereas one with very little time to run may be difficult to sell and thus warrant little or no premium. By contrast, when the property market is in the doldrums, a tenant anxious to sell may even pay his or her buyer a 'reverse premium' to take over the lease. It is unusual for a premium to be called for by a landlord on the grant of a new lease; a tenant may expect instead to have to bear his or her legal costs for granting it. Where a tenant is required by a new lease to spend money on fitting out the premises, it may be appropriate for him or her to ask for a rent-free period as recompense.

Length of lease

When does the lease come to an end? Are there any likely hindrances to a renewal? Does the landlord have the right to end it before it runs out?

You will minimise your responsibilities by acquiring premises on as short a lease as possible. This is not difficult in the case of buying a suitable existing lease. But what are your rights if you want to stay on at the premises once the lease has come to an end?

Ideally your lease would give you a right to a new lease if you so wish. However, landlords may not be prepared to tie their hands in this way. A tenant of business premises does have a right to apply to the court for the grant of a new lease (with some minor exceptions) but the landlord may object on certain grounds. It will thus never be certain that a tenant will succeed in obtaining a new lease against his landlord's opposition. In practice, however, the vast majority of such cases are settled by negotiation. A free leaflet, *Business Leases and Security of Tenure*, is available from the Department of the Environment.★

Selling the lease

You may find that circumstances force you to sub-let, surrender a lease early, or to 'assign' it to a new tenant. Check the lease particularly carefully for your rights in these situations. The landlord will want to vet any prospective buyer (known as an 'assignee'), and although landlords cannot unreasonably refuse to allow a lease to be assigned to a new tenant, they can impose severe financial and other preconditions that have to be met. A particularly nasty precondition to beware of is that even after assigning the lease you could remain liable for any rent unpaid by future tenants.

Permitted use

Is it adequate for your present and future business use? Can the landlord be required to consent to a change in permitted use? Is the marketability of the lease likely to be restricted when you want to sell it?

Repairs

Whose responsibility are they – if yours, is there any cap on the amount you might have to pay? Ensure that there is a full description of the premises, to establish the limits of liability for repairs. Do they include the foundations? The roof? The loadbearing walls?

Unless the landlord is fully responsible for repairs and the cost of repairs, make sure that you have a full structural survey of the premises carried out before you buy. Money spent on repairing someone else's property is money you will not see again. If the survey sounds expensive, talk to the surveyor about a negotiated fee. You do not want a lengthy catalogue listing features that you can see for yourself, nor a full unlimited guarantee on which you could sue if the surveyor missed anything. What you want is a realistic guide to the value of the property and what you must do to it soon, what you can risk leaving for a while, and what is unimportant structurally. Also ask the surveyor to verify any information given by the landlord, such as the amount of business rates.

Alterations

What kind of alterations can be carried out without permission from the landlord? Does the landlord's permission have to be obtained for business signs? If the property is an older one which you will have to refurbish at your own expense, you will be increasing its value to the owner, so you may be able to negotiate a cheaper rent.

Services

Check that there will be no difficulties with the mains services, that there will be enough electric power, water, gas, and also adequate drainage, and no difficulties about the telephone.

Somebody who is a low user of water should ask for the supply to be metered instead of being charged at a fixed rate.

Fire prevention

You now have legal obligations to take various fire precautions even if you have only one employee.

Premises require a fire certificate if they are used as a place of work, a shop, factory or office where more than 20 people are employed, or more than 10 people elsewhere than on the ground floor; or if explosives or highly flammable substances are stored there.

If you are moving into previously occupied premises, find out whether there is a current fire certificate, and if so, whether it covers your operations. If your occupancy constitutes a change of conditions because of structural alterations, a change of use, or change in the number of persons working, you will need a new certificate.

Your local fire safety officer grants the certificate if he or she is satisfied, after inspecting the premises, that all necessary precautions have been taken.

Consult your fire safety officer before you clinch the deal for any premises: if your work means installing a number of fire escapes, fire doors, or new flooring, this may prove to be too expensive to be worthwhile.

If you fail to comply with your fire safety officer's directions, you can be prosecuted, and in the worst case, closed down without notice.

You may also find that until you have satisfied the demands of fire prevention, you will be refused insurance or any other kind of permission that may also be required.

Even if you do not need a fire certificate, if you employ someone, then you are specifically required to assess the risks from fire at your workplace and to take the necessary precautions. This may include fire detection equipment and alarms, firefighting equipment, fire escapes, emergency doors and lighting and ensuring that there is someone competent to implement them. So it makes sense to consult your local fire safety officer in any case.

Planning permission

Make sure that the premises you choose already have the planning permission that you will need. Otherwise you will have to apply to the local authority's planning department for permission to make alterations or to change the use of the premises. Obtaining this can take months (and there are fees to be paid). If you take the local authority's planners into your confidence from the start, they may prove remarkably helpful, and eager not to thwart a new business, unless there are overwhelming objections to the plans you put forward.

If you intend to start from a green-field site and build on it, planning permission will take much longer, and is only one of the obstacles to be overcome.

A free booklet, *Planning Permission: A Guide for Business*, is available from the Department of the Environment.★

Rate relief and concessions

If you are not tied to any one area and can set up anywhere, you may be better off in an assisted area, where you may sometimes get subsidised accommodation.

English Partnerships★ is a government agency with a remit to release the potential of derelict and vacant land throughout England. It can offer various types of support, such as loan guarantees, to projects that meet this aim. In some areas it undertakes the development itself, making commercial and industrial premises available for rent. It operates from six regional offices, with a head office in London.

Many local authorities are prepared to give initial rate relief to new businesses and those relocating themselves into the area. Get in touch with the planning department or the economic unit of your local authority about these or other concessions.

If you intend to set up a business in a rural area, the local Rural Development Commission office may know of small properties, converted barns, or other accommodation available for rent.

Sublet premises

If you need only a modest amount of space, you may be able to find an existing business which has spare capacity, and is glad to reduce its overheads by subletting to you. The kind of company to look for is one in a similar but not competing line of business: the association could even result in a partnership.

Chapter 6

Squaring up to accounts

The figures that your business generates are an index of its health and growth. Many people in a small business seem to be positively scared of them and keep no continuous control.

It is not good enough to monitor the state of health of the business by the annual accounts, which are not available until the following year is well advanced. If anything is then found to be amiss, it may well be too late to put it right.

You may feel that if you employ an accountant, it is his or her job to keep an eye on the figures, on the why-keep-a-dog-and-bark-yourself? principle. But an accountant should rather be thought of as a doctor who cannot compel you to look after your business health properly, but can only diagnose the sickness resulting from your imprudence. He or she certainly cannot cure it once it has become terminal.

So, do not be scared of your accounts and take an informed interest in what the figures show you. You should know at the end of each month, if not every week, whether it has been a profitable one, and whether you have enough money, in hand or on tap, to cover your expenses for the coming month. Your calculations need not be very elaborate: quite rough monthly accounts, backed up by an accountant's quarterly report, will enable you to stay in control.

For advice on how to find an accountant, see page 43.

What can you do for yourself?

Your accountant could, of course, carry out your monthly monitoring for you; but it is most unlikely that your new, small business could afford the expense. If you do this work for yourself, you will be in a position to know, at all times, what is happening to your business, and to forecast what is going to happen next.

What is more, you will then have no trouble in understanding the accountant's quarterly reports, and relating them to your own day-to-day experience. Even if you prefer to have your accountant do all the figure work, you must be able to make sense of the reports that are prepared for you.

Keeping business records

There are excellent reasons why you should keep good business records: because the Inland Revenue and Customs and Excise (for VAT) require it, because your bank manager may require regular information, and because you will save your accountant's time (charged for by the hour). But the most important reason is that properly kept accounts, summarised at the end of each month and coupled with a stocktake or an estimate of the value of your stock, will give you the up-to-date knowledge of your affairs which you will need to spot danger signs while there is still time to put things right, and to plan ahead for further improvements or expansion, if things go well.

Who keeps the books?

Although all modern double-entry bookkeeping follows the same general pattern, no two firms' sets of books are identical: every business has some individual aspects which must be recorded, and every businessman or businesswoman has his or her own notions of which of these records should be monitored.

So get your accountant, who understands your particular requirements, to set up your books for you, and to teach you how to keep them. He or she will probably do so willingly, for it is to his or her advantage, as well as yours, to be presented with clear, well-kept books to deal with. Or, better still, ask your bookkeeper to teach a member of your family who can relieve you of the task. It is not difficult, and it will probably be some time before your business demands the services of a full-time trained bookkeeper.

You can also teach yourself the elements of bookkeeping from one of a variety of books on the subject, but be sure to acquire this skill before you start up, because you will not have time afterwards.

The records you must keep

Business records may be kept and presented in a variety of ways, and depend very much on the type of business for their format.

However, one feature is common to all systems: they must be backed by evidence that the receipts and payments recorded have actually been made. So be sure to keep safely all of the following:

- cheque-book stubs
- cancelled cheques (tell the bank to return them to you)
- bank paying-in books (use these, not paying in slips)
- bank statements (make sure that you have separate accounts – even if they are at the same bank – for business and private life, whether you are a sole trader or partnership or company)
- copies of your own invoices, receipts and delivery notes
- your suppliers' invoices, receipts and delivery notes
- receipts, wherever possible, for minor purchases made in cash
- copies of all VAT returns.

You should also keep records of any private money going in and out of the business – for example, a loan from an investor, any money that you draw out to live on. A useful guide is the Inland Revenue leaflet *Self-Assessment: A guide to keeping records for the self-employed*, available from tax offices (in the phone book under 'Inland Revenue').

The books

For keeping accounts, even at their simplest, you must keep several books. The 'books' need not be paper-based: computer accounting software for small businesses is now widely available – but if you keep your records on computer you must still keep the original paper record of your sales, purchases and other similar transactions.

The cash book is the most basic account book. It records all your payments and receipts made by cheque (for this purpose cheques are regarded as cash) or in ready money.

Some businesses are purely cash ones – this means that, whether you are buying or selling, payment is made immediately. If yours is not one of these, and you buy and sell with payment at a later date, you will need two further books – a sales day book for recording your sales invoices as they are sent out, and a purchases day book in which are recorded your purchases of goods and services.

This last book, which is all-important, will be of the kind called an analysis book, ruled with a number of vertical columns, in which you classify your different kinds of expenditure: materials, direct labour and the various sorts of overheads. If you are working on paper, rather than computer, be sure to get a book with enough columns; how many you will need depends on your particular expenses, and on how minutely you want to break the figures down.

By adding up each column every month, you will see exactly how much each of your business expenses came to. The total of these totals will give you your whole month's costs. If you are registered for VAT, you will have a VAT column in both your sales and your purchases books, to record the amount of VAT that other people pay you, and that which you pay; you will need this information for your quarterly VAT return.

If you employ anyone you must keep a record of wages paid, showing gross earnings, deductions for income tax, National Insurance, any pension scheme, any other deductions, net pay and the employer's National Insurance contributions. You can obtain a proprietary wages book system from a business stationer. If you decide to use a computer in your business, you can buy software that will attend to the wages record for you.

The petty cash book is a record of small out-of-pocket expenses paid by you or your staff in the course of work, such as fares, taxis or the window cleaner. The money is paid out of a float drawn at intervals from the bank (and duly recorded in the cash and purchases books). The petty cash book is on the same lines as the purchases book, with columns for different types of expenditure.

Slightly more advanced bookkeeping

As your business expands and becomes more complex, you will need to start keeping ledgers.

The sales ledger is based on the sales day book, and records the individual accounts of each of your customers, showing how much he or she has bought in any given period and the date of payments.

This enables you to keep an eye on slow payers. It is also invaluable in planning future marketing strategy. It may show, for instance, that 80 per cent of your trade is with a few customers placing substantial orders, and 20 per cent is with a large number of small customers. You will then have to decide whether to go on accepting small orders whose costs are high in relation to profits, in the hope that the small customers may be encouraged to grow into bigger ones.

The purchases ledger is based on the purchases day book, and records your transactions with each of your suppliers. It shows which of them are getting the largest share of your custom; these will be the ones most likely to give credit or offer generous cash discounts.

The general ledger records impersonal payments, that is, the sale and purchase of equipment, rent and rates, services, and so on, and the totals of income and expenditure.

These ledgers are the foundation for a double-entry bookkeeping system. A full explanation of this would require a book to itself, but the principle on which it is based is simple: every transaction must be recorded twice, once as a debit and once as a credit, according to whether it is regarded from a buyer's or a seller's point of view.

Every sale you make represents a debit entry to your customer in the sales ledger and a credit to you in the sales account in the general ledger: when the customer pays, this appears as a debit entry in the cash book and a credit entry in the sales ledger.

Every purchase you make from your supplier is a credit entry for him or her in your purchases ledger and a debit for you in the general ledger. When you pay up, this is recorded as a credit in your cash book and a debit for the supplier in the purchases ledger.

Using what your figures tell you

With all these records, you are in a position to make calculations showing how your business is progressing. The all-important one is your monthly net profit. To arrive at this you need to draw up a monthly trading account and a profit and loss account. The monthly trading account shows the gross profits of your business. You calculate it by adding together your month's labour and materials costs, and the difference between the value of your opening and closing stocks, and subtracting this from the total monthly sales figure.

Jane's product sells at £20 per unit; of this, her materials cost £10 and labour costs £2. Her overheads are £800 a month. Using the sales, purchase and labour totals shown by her books, Jane draws up a trading account, thus:

Jane's trading account for one month

	£		£
Opening stock		Sales	4,000
(100 units @ £12)	1,200		
Purchases of materials			
(200 @£10)	2,000		
Labour (200 @ £2)	400		
	3,600		
Less closing stock			
(80 @ £12)	960		
	2,640		
Balance, i.e. gross profit	1,360		
	4,000		4,000

Jane has valued her stock at materials and labour costs only: overheads do not enter the calculation until the next step, the monthly estimated net profit. This is how it looks in Jane's case:

Jane's profit and loss account

	£		£
Overheads	800	Gross profit	1,360
Balance i.e. net profit	560		
	1,360		1,360

This is the most basic way of drawing up a profit and loss account. It can be combined with the trading account in a single calculation. There is no special presentation that must be followed.

You can make it more informative by making it more complex: you can isolate and thus highlight items of overheads or other factors that you particularly want to keep an eye on, for instance, the cost of power consumption. Or, because power is a cost that varies with the volume of production, you could choose to treat it as a materials purchase, rather than an overhead.

Here we have assumed that Jane's enterprise is a limited company and her salary is therefore one of the overheads. If she were a sole trader, her remuneration (say, £350 a month) would not be included in the overheads, which would then be £450 a month, and the month's net profit before tax would be £910, and would constitute Jane's taxable income.

However, you may have a profit and loss account that looks as healthy as this one, and still run out of funds, because it does not show that at any one time you may not actually have in hand all the money due to you. If your suppliers demand cash on delivery while your customers will only place orders on 30- or 60-day credit terms, and your expanding business is demanding additional unforeseen expenditure, you have got a cash flow problem.

Cash flow forecasting

The drawing up of a cash flow forecast has already been explained in Chapter 2. In the examples here, the tables are considerably simplified; they ignore VAT and assume equal monthly overheads.

Jane's latest cash flow forecast looks like this (figures in brackets denote a deficit):

Month	Jan	Feb	Mar	Apr	May
	£	£	£	£	£
Opening bank balance/[overdraft]	[3,000]	[2,200]	[1,400]	[600]	200
Payments:					
purchases	2,000	2,000	2,000	2,000	2,000
labour	400	400	400	400	400
overheads	800	800	800	800	800
Maximum borrowing requirement	6,200	5,400	4,600	3,800	3,000
Receipts from sales	4,000	4,000	4,000	4,000	4,000
Closing balance/[overdraft]	[2,200]	[1,400]	[600]	200	1,000

Jane has now been asked to take on a regular order for another 200 units a month, but with payment only after 90 days. This means another machine at £500, plus additional part-time labour costs, and it will take two months to build up the manufacturing capacity. In order to be in a position to decide whether to accept the order, Jane prepares another forecast, which looks like this: (figures in brackets denote a deficit)

Month	Jun	Jul	Aug	Sep	Oct	Nov	Dec
Products made	200	300	400	400	400	400	400
	£	£	£	£	£	£	£
Opening balance/ [overdraft]	1,000	300	[1,300]	[2,900]	[4,500]	[4,100]	[1,700]
Payment:							
purchases	3,000	4,000	4,000	4,000	4,000	4,000	4,000
labour	400	800	800	800	800	800	800
overheads	800	800	800	800	800	800	800
Capital expenditure	500						
Maximum borrowing requirement	3,700	5,300	6,900	8,500	10,100	9,700	7,300
Receipts from sales	4,000	4,000	4,000	4,000	6,000	8,000	8,000
Closing balance/ [overdraft]	300	[1,300]	[2,900]	[4,500]	[4,100]	[1,700]	700

This forecast shows her that if she accepts the order under these conditions, she will be overdrawn for five months, and will need a further investment of around £4,500 for three months, to pay for the additional costs. The bank might well be willing, on the basis of this profitable order, to lend the money to a customer who had already succeeded in repaying an overdraft of £3,000. To minimise her borrowing requirement, Jane might be able to persuade her suppliers to agree to a delayed payment, and might also be able to dovetail this payment into those months when no major overheads were due.

In order to keep the example simple, two other factors have been excluded: the cost of additional power consumption resulting from increased production, and the interest payable on bank loans or overdrafts; but a rough calculation is all that is wanted at this stage.

Jane's experience shows that for a small, newly established firm, a large order, unaccompanied by prompt payment, can be a disaster if there is no means of stretching resources to cover the expenditure demanded by the additional output. By making a forecast on similar lines, you will be able to see how your money supply will relate to expenditure.

Having discovered what your volume of production is to be in the next six months or so, your next task is to discover at which point you will begin to make a profit.

Break-even point

Every business has a break-even point, at which it is producing just enough for the receipts to balance the costs. Before this point is reached, the business is working at a loss; when it is passed, the business is showing a profit.

In a manufacturing business the break-even point is measured in units of production; in a service business it is measured in the number of paid hours worked.

Fixed and variable costs

The costs of manufacturing anything can be divided into two categories: fixed and variable. *Fixed costs* are the ones which remain the same whatever the amount you manufacture: the overheads and, in the short term, labour. *Variable costs* are those which vary with the amount you manufacture, such as materials and power.

Some costs are partly fixed and partly variable, for example power, which you are bound to use to some extent even without manufacturing anything: they should be split, in calculations, into their fixed and variable elements. However, in the example that follows, power has, for the sake of simplicity, been treated as an overhead.

In the case of George, another manufacturer, the relationship between his volume of production (number of units made and sold in a month) and his profitability is shown in the table opposite.

These figures can be expressed in a graph. The horizontal axis represents the number of units produced, the vertical axis represents money. On this are plotted George's selling price and total cost at each volume of production. The two lines intersect at the

George's profit at each volume of production

Units made	Variable cost	Fixed cost	Total cost	Receipts from sales	Profit/ [loss]
20	200	1,200	1,400	400	[1,000]
60	600	1,200	1,800	1,200	[600]
100	1,000	1,200	2,200	2,000	[200]
140	1,400	1,200	2,600	2,800	200

point at which production is 120 units: this is where he is just covering his costs, and beyond this, he will begin to make a profit.

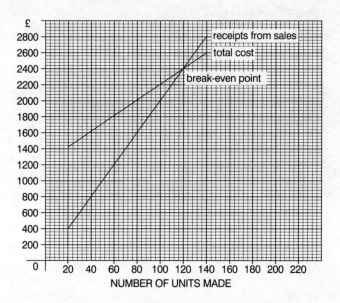

A calculation and simple graph like this will enable you to plan your volume of production intelligently in relation to your financial resources. You can use it to explore the way in which fixed costs, variable costs, sales prices and profits affect each other. For instance, you may wish to expand manufacture to an extent which will increase your fixed costs: can you maintain profits, bearing in mind your probable increase in variable costs?

Never forget to revise your cash flow forecast when you expect a change in circumstances, particularly if you are thinking of expanding production in search of higher sales.

Balance sheet

At any time after starting up, you may want to analyse your deployment of your resources: the balance sheet constitutes such an analysis. You will need – and any substantial lender will require – not just a year-end balance sheet, but also intermediate ones, or the details for them at regular intervals. You can then observe what the trend is in any particular matter that you want to analyse.

A balance sheet shows the financial state of the business at a given date and is based on the account balances in the ledgers at that date. It takes account of what the business owns (its assets), and of what it owes (its liabilities). Both of these may be subdivided into fixed and current balances:

- Fixed liabilities are debts which are repayable over a long period of time.
- Current liabilities are those which must be repaid in the short term, such as debts to suppliers, overdrafts, and interest on loans.
- Fixed assets are property such as land, buildings, plant, machinery and vehicles. (These need to be revalued periodically, and their book value adjusted; land and buildings tend to increase in value with inflation, while plant, machinery and vehicles depreciate and have to be replaced. It is useful to set up a sinking fund or reserve for an eventual replacement cost.)
- Current assets include customers' book debts, the value of any stock held, and money in hand or in the bank.
- Quick assets are narrow current assets represented by money; by assets which can be quickly converted to money, such as Stock Exchange securities; and by some short-term book debts, where these are by customers in good standing. Raw materials are not included nor, generally, are finished goods.

From the figures for assets and liabilities you can make several kinds of analysis. For example, you can look at the ability of your business to meet its commitments. Is it solvent? That is, would it be able to pay its outside creditors in full (if necessary by selling all its assets)?

It is easier to compare balance sheet positions if you convert the actual figures into a ratio or percentage of solvency.

Another test of solvency is to see whether the business, as a going concern, can meet its current liabilities out of its current assets; again, it is usual to express this in the form of a ratio. This 'current ratio' should usually be rather better than 1:1, because not all current assets may be easily saleable, so a margin of safety is prudent.

The acid test is to see how far current liabilities can be paid out of quick assets; expressed as the 'quick ratio', this will be less than the current ratio, and often less than 1:1. In all these tests you must use up-to-date realistic sale values for the assets.

Your accountant will be able to advise you about choosing the ratios that are appropriate for your own particular business, and can also tell you about some other useful analyses that you can make.

In George's case, his resources have been as follows: £3,000 capital; an overdraft facility of £2,000, of which he is at present using only £1,200; a medium-term bank loan of £2,500 to buy plant and machinery. His profit has not been taken out, but kept in reserve to

George's balance sheet at 1 January 1998

	£	£	£
ASSETS			
Fixed assets:			
plant and machinery	6,500		
motor vehicles	4,000		
	10,500		
Less hire-purchase debt	2,000	8,500	
Current assets			
stock	1,000		
debtors	2,500	3,500	12,000
LIABILITIES:			
Medium-term bank loan		2,500	
Current liabilities:			
creditors	2,800		
overdraft	1,200	4,000	6,500
TOTAL NET ASSETS			5,500
Resources to generate these net assets are:			
George's capital introduced into business		3,000	
George's undrawn profits left in business		2,500	
			5,500

be used to buy additional plant and to provide additional working capital. It would be astute to invest all his reserves, if these were not needed immediately, which would then be entered as 'investments' on the asset side of the balance.

Assuming that George has used realistic values for the assets, then, even in a forced sale, the business is solvent. But it cannot meet current liabilities out of current assets: there is a £500 shortfall (£4,000 as against £3,500). Even less can it meet current liabilities out of 'quick' assets: there is a £1,500 shortfall, so this balance sheet is weak. We know, however, that George has £800 unused overdraft facility, and he may possibly have extra personal funds, which he could introduce. But, on the face of it, the business depends on the continued renewal of overdraft arrangements, which makes it vulnerable.

This is only one balance sheet: a whole series of them might show that this single one gives an unusually poor impression of the business. One balance sheet a year cannot ever be informative enough.

There are many ways of presenting a balance sheet, and individual items can be more closely analysed; for instance, stock can be divided into finished stock and raw materials. If you are making your balance sheet, keep it simple to begin with; if an accountant does it for you, be sure that it is done in a form that you can understand.

The very basic balance sheet shown does not take account of the difference between a sole trader (or partnership) and a limited company. In practice, the balance sheet of a company would have to be drawn up rather differently. Its capital would have to be shown among the liabilities, because it belongs not to the company, but to its shareholders. The same is true of the net profit on the trading account: it must ultimately be distributed among the shareholders. In a sole-trader firm or partnership, the capital investment and the profits are owned by the firm and are, therefore, assets.

Chapter 7

Taxation and the small business

When you set up in business for yourself, you come up against taxation in several different ways. You may pay:

- income tax on your business profits, or on your share of them, if you are a sole trader or partnership
- corporation tax on your profits if yours is a limited company, and if you are in the happy situation of making some profits in excess of the directors' salaries or remuneration
- value added tax (VAT)
- National Insurance contributions.

All taxes are liable to change at any time, not only with each year's Budget. Major changes are usually publicised in the national press, and you can ask your accountant to keep you up to date. Your local tax enquiry centre (in the phone book under 'Inland Revenue') can be consulted at any time for the latest figures.

The first thing to do

You need to inform the relevant tax authorities that you are starting up. The taxes above are administered by three different government departments or agencies:

- the Inland Revenue administers income tax, corporation tax and some National Insurance contributions
- the Contributions Agency deals with other National Insurance contributions
- Customs and Excise administers VAT.

Fortunately, you do not need to inform all of these departments separately. Instead, ask for a copy of the leaflet *Starting your own business?* (CWL1) which is available from the local offices of any of the three bodies above. This contains a form CWF1 which you should complete and send off to the Contributions Agency at the address shown on the form: it will pass on your details to the other tax authorities. You may then be sent further forms to complete, for example if you need or want to register for VAT.

As well as giving an introduction to the taxes you might have to pay, the leaflet also lists many other useful leaflets, helplines, and further sources of advice. If you have access to the Internet, many of these are now available through the Government Internet site at http://www.open.gov.uk

Income tax

Directors of companies

If yours is a limited company, you, as one of its full-time directors, are an employee: you therefore pay income tax on your salary and on any bonus under the PAYE system, like any other employee. At the start of each trading year, you determine what your annual salary is to be, and you pay it to yourself monthly or weekly. Each time, you deduct income tax according to instructions provided by the Inland Revenue, to whom you send the deducted amounts, together with National Insurance contributions from you and your employees. These payroll deductions are usually sent in every month. Sometimes they may be paid in on a quarterly basis.

Salaries need not necessarily be fixed at the start of the trading year; a review may take place part way through the year. If, at the end of the trading year, the company accounts show a profit in excess of your salary or remuneration, you have the option of taking some or all of this profit as additional salary or bonus, and deducting tax from it. If there is another director (or directors), then it will be necessary to decide how to apportion such a bonus.

You also have the opportunity of paying, out of the profits, a dividend – either instead of, or as well as a bonus. Dividends are payable to the company's shareholders (who are often also the directors), in proportion to the shares held. Where shareholders are few, payment by dividends can be attractive because, unlike salary, there is no National Insurance to pay on them. There may be an advantage in paying a dividend to the shareholders before the end of the trading year: your accountant should be able to advise you on this.

Whatever part of the profits is not taken in salary, is liable for (or, in Inland Revenue jargon, 'charged to') corporation tax. It is for you, in consultation with your accountant, to decide whether it is to your advantage to pay more income tax or more corporation tax.

Sole traders and partnerships

If you are a sole trader, or a partnership, there is no decision to be made: the whole of your business profits are treated as sole trader's or partners' income and taxed accordingly (under Schedule D); corporation tax does not apply.

Choosing your accounting year

A firm's accounts are made up annually. This does not apply to the first trading period, which may be shorter than a year, or longer. But it is usual to nominate the day of the year on which you first close your books as your annual accounting date, and to go on using this day as the end of the trading year for as long as the firm continues in business. It is for you to decide which day is to be your year's end. You may make it coincide with the end of the tax (fiscal) year, i.e. 5 April, or with the end of the calendar year; or you may choose any other date which suits you. Note that, if your year-end is 31 March, the Inland Revenue will allow you to treat it as ending on 5 April, which simplifies the tax calculations.

The Inland Revenue suggests that if yours is a seasonal business, you should arrange to end your year in a slack period; your accountant may suggest a date soon after 5 April because, as will be explained later, this gives you the longest initial period for paying your taxes.

Declaring your profits

You have to declare your income, expenses and profits on your tax return each year. Under the new system of 'self-assessment' which took full effect in the 1996–7 tax year, you are now responsible for assessing your own tax liability. When you complete your tax return, you are telling the Inland Revenue 'this is what my tax position is'. You may ask it to calculate the tax on your behalf by doing the arithmetic – providing you send in your tax return by 30 September after the end of the tax year– but essentially you collect the information needed to assess your tax position, and summarise this via the tax return.

You do not need to send in any accounts, unless your business is very complex or very large. But whether or not you intend to calculate your own tax you need to give detailed information on the tax return itself (though if your turnover is below £15,000 a year you need enter just your turnover, allowable expenses and the resulting profit). When you are setting up your bookkeeping system, it will simplify matters if it is consistent with the Inland Revenue tax return. Ask your accountant, or get leaflet SA3 *Self-assessment: a guide to keeping records for the self-employed* from any tax office.

Even if you do not have to send in accounts, you still have to keep them. You have a legal duty to keep various records for a min-imum length of time (covered in the leaflet mentioned above) and your tax inspector has the right (although it is seldom exercised) to ask for complete records of the whole of the firm's payments and receipts (including what has been drawn for private expenditure), supported by invoices, receipts, bank records and statements, pay-ing-in books and cheque stubs.

You do not have to use an accountant or other tax adviser. It is not a requirement of the tax system, and the Inland Revenue has helplines and tax enquiry centres which can be very helpful. Consumers' Association publishes TaxCalc, a computer program which helps you complete your tax return and work out your tax bill. However, there are advantages in consulting a professional. As well as completing your tax return for you, he or she ought to be able to guide you on what expenses and allowances you can claim to reduce your tax bill. See page 43 for how to find an accountant or tax adviser.

Even if you use an accountant, you must keep an eye on what is being done in your name. Accountants are fallible, and you are still responsible for declaring your income correctly. In particular, note that there are important deadlines which you must meet or risk paying penalties. For example, you must send in your tax return by 31 January after the end of the tax year, and (in most cases) make payments of tax 'on account' on each 31 July and 31 January.

Allowances on capital expenditure

Capital expenditure is money spent on plant, buildings, machinery, vehicles, and anything else that has an enduring benefit for the business and does not need to be renewed every year. It is not in itself, tax deductible, but you may qualify for 'capital allowances'.

Capital allowances are calculated by putting the cost of the plant or machinery you buy into a 'pool of expenditure'. Each year, you can claim up to 25 per cent of the value of the pool as a 'writing-down allowance' which can be deducted from your profits for that year. The pool is reduced by what you claim: what's left is the 'written-down value' and becomes your pool for the start of the next accounting year. Any purchases for the next year are added to the pool, and at the end of the year you can claim 25 per cent of what the pool is then worth. Note that you can claim less than the full writing-down allowance: this is worth doing if your profits are less than the potential allowance.

If you sell something on which you have claimed capital allowance, the proceeds must be deducted from your pool of expenditure before working out your writing-down allowance for the year in which you sell. If the proceeds of all the items you sell come to more than the value of the pool, the excess (which is called a 'balancing charge') is added to your profits for the year and taxed.

Most expenditure goes into one common pool. However, any car costing more than £12,000 must be kept in its own separate pool, with a maximum writing-down allowance of £3,000 a year. Items used partly for business, partly for private use, should also be pooled separately, since you can claim only the proportion of the expenditure which is in line with business use. You can elect for many capital items with an expected life of less than five years – computers, say – to be treated as 'short-life assets'. Each one is put into its own pool of expenditure. As long as use of them stops within the five years, you get immediate tax relief for any disposal (instead of having to wait until the business ceases, as you do with assets in your main pool).

Capital allowances can be a complicated business, and it would be worth consulting an accountant or tax adviser if you are thinking of a substantial capital purchase. Sometimes the Government makes available a higher initial allowance instead of the normal writing-down allowance. For example, small and medium-sized businesses could claim a first-year allowance of 50 per cent on expenditure on some machinery and plant (not cars) in the 12 months ending on 1 July 1998.

Deductible expenses

A proportion of those expenses which are not capital expenditure and which are incurred wholly and exclusively for the purposes of carrying on the business can be set off against tax. There is no definitive list of 'allowable' expenses, but items of expenditure which are generally allowed include:

- wages (including pensions, etc.) of staff employed in the business (you can claim for wages paid to members of your family but only if they are genuinely employed)
- expenses of business travel (but not of going to and from home to the main place of work)
- interest on loans taken out for the acquisition or running of a business
- interest charges on hire-purchase of capital equipment
- hire or leasing of equipment
- insurance premiums
- bad debts
- subscriptions to trade and professional associations
- general overheads, such as telephone, heating and lighting, advertising, stationery and postage
- accountancy fees, bank charges, etc.

Bear in mind that to be tax-deductible, the wages a husband pays to his wife (or vice versa) must be commensurate with the work she or he actually does, and paid at a fair commercial rate.

If your house or telephone are used partly for your business, you may claim against tax a proportion of the expenses (rent, council tax, telephone rental, light, heating and so on). But if you claim half the council tax, say, as a business expense because, for the period of your business, only half the house is residential and the other half is commercial, then when later on you sell the house, there will be a potential capital gains tax liability on half of the appreciation in value during that time. However, see 'Capital profits' (page 120) for reliefs which could reduce, or even eliminate, the bill.

In the case of a car, some proportion of its cost (corresponding to the proportion of business use) may be the subject of a claim to capital allowances, and a similar proportion of the running costs may be claimed as a deductible business expense. You must, therefore, keep a record of the business mileage and the total mileage. If your turnover is low, you can work out the costs on a 'cost per business mile' basis, provided the rate per mile does not exceed that in the 'Fixed Profit Car Scheme' scales, published periodically by the Inland Revenue.

Tax relief for business losses

If a sole trader (or partnership) who has been in business for a number of years makes a loss, under current rules the loss can be set against any other income the trader receives in the same or the next tax year (provided he or she is still in the same business then). Such a loss can also be set against other income for the previous tax year (even if he or she was not then in business). If losses exceed income, the excess can be set against any capital gains for the given year.

Losses incurred in the first four years of trading may be claimed to be set against wages or other income received in the three years before the trading loss was incurred: a part of the tax paid during that period may then be refunded.

These are useful and valuable options. The sole trader can also choose to carry the losses forward to future business years to set against future profits. There would need to be special reasons to choose to do that: one reason would be that in the past he or she had not had much income and therefore had paid little or no tax. Early trading losses might then be more useful if set against future profits.

How business income tax is assessed

The tax for sole traders and partnerships is generally based on profits for the accounting period ending during the current tax year. However, special rules apply to the first – and sometimes the second – tax year of your being in business:

- *first tax year* (i.e. the year in which the business commences): tax is based on the profits from day one of trading up to 5 April. If the first accounting period ends later than 5 April, a proportion of the profits is calculated on a time basis

- *second tax year*: tax is based on the profits for the 12 months up to the end of the accounting period which ends in that tax year. If you have not been in business for a full year by then, tax is based on profits for the first 12 months. Sometimes there is no accounting date in the second tax year. This would be the case if your first accounting period lasted for longer than a year and happened to straddle three tax years – if you started up in January 1996, say, planning to close your books for the first time in July 1997. In this case, your second year's tax bill would be based on the actual profits of the tax year, that is, in the example above, on 12/18 of the profits of the accounting period.
- *third and subsequent years*: tax is based on profits for the 12 months up to the end of the accounting year which ends in that tax year (i.e. on your profits for your last accounting period).

An example will help clarify this. Tom started on 6 September 1997 fixing 5 September as his accounting year-end. In his first trading year, his taxable profits were £13,715; in his second, they were £14,200; in his third, £16,000.

tax year (6-5 April)	assessment period from	to	taxable profits £
1997–8	6.9.97	5.4.98	8,000 ($^7/_{12}$ of 13,715)
1998–9	6.9.97	5.9.98	13,715
1999–2000	6.9.98	5.9.99	14,200
2000–1	6.9.99	5.9.2000	16,000

This shows that a new business's profits for the first two years are often assessed on the basis of the first 12 months of trading. Although there is a special relief, called overlap relief, which compensates for this, it is available only when you cease trading or change your accounting date. Generally speaking, therefore, the first 12 months' profits should be kept as low as possible for tax purposes or you will have to choose your year-end carefully.

When tax is payable
When the first tax bill on your business profits is due depends on when in the tax year you start up. You may have a small bill to pay

fairly soon, or you might have a longer tax-free period and then a big bill to settle in one go.

You have to notify your tax office that you have taxable income by 5 October after the end of the tax year, following which you will be sent a tax return (if you haven't had one already). Under the new system of self-assessment, the tax return enables you (or your accountant) to work out any tax due, which must be paid by 31 January or, if later, three months after the date on the return. You can ask the Inland Revenue to work out the tax for you if you send back your return by 30 September following the end of the tax year in question.

After that, tax is due in three instalments, on 31 January during the tax year in question, 31 July just after the end of the tax year, and the following 31 January. The first two payments are 'payments on account' and are based on your tax bill for the previous year (or an estimate if your first trading period has not yet ended). The third and final 'balancing payment' is due the following 31 January at the same time as the tax return and will cover any tax outstanding. So if you pay tax for your first year on 31 January following the end of the tax year, the first instalment for the following year will be due at the same time.

Your choice of accounting date will affect the gap between making your profits and paying tax on them. Tom makes his first tax payment by 31 January 1999, i.e. only five months after the end of his first trading year on 5 September 1998. If his accounting date were 30 April 1998, the payment would not be due until nine months after his year-end. Either way he should budget for the fact that his January 1999 payment will include not only his tax so far, but also his first payment on account for the 1998–9 tax year.

Partnerships

The profits of a partnership are calculated in the same way as for a sole trader. The taxable profits are then split up between the partners, for tax purposes, in line with the profit-sharing agreement in force for that year. Each partner's tax bill then depends on his or her other income, reliefs and allowances. So if, for example, the profits are £40,000 and there are two partners sharing the profits equally, the £40,000 will be divided equally between them. But if one partner pays tax at the basic rate, and the other is a higher-rate taxpayer (because he or she has lots of other income, say) the tax each pays on their share will be different. In effect, each partner is treated as if they run their own individual business based on their share of the partnership profits. Partners are responsible for tax only on their own share of the profits (see Chapter 3).

Corporation tax: limited companies

Most of what has been said about income tax on business profits (also known as Schedule D income tax) applies to the payment of corporation tax. Here are the main differences between the two.

Corporation tax is the tax which companies pay on their profits. There are two different rates:

- a full rate – 31 per cent in 1997–8
- a small-company rate – 21 per cent in 1997–8

A small company is currently defined as one whose annual profits are £300,000 or less: up to this amount, the lower tax rate of 21 per cent is charged on all profits. Above this, the rate of tax gradually increases, according to a simple formula, until at £1.5 million the full rate of 31 per cent applies, on all profits.

Note that for 1997–8, the 21 per cent small-company rate of corporation tax is less than the 23 per cent basic rate of tax applying for sole traders and partnerships. In previous years, the two rates have tended to be the same. This differential, if it continues in future, may in some cases make setting up as a company rather more attractive than it has been in the past (see Chapter 3). But this is an area in which you would be wise to get advice from an accountant.

How not to pay corporation tax

Another material difference between a sole trader and a company lies in the fact that the salaries paid to company directors are a business cost, like any other salaries, and so are deducted in calculating profits. As the directors' remuneration need not be fixed until the results of the year's trading are known, it may be advantageous to a small company to pay out all its trading surplus as directors' salaries, on which they pay individual income tax. (For remuneration to qualify as a deduction, however, the company must be able to show that it was paid or was made available 'wholly and exclusively for the purpose of the trade'.) Any part of the surplus that is not paid out is known as 'retained profit' and is subjected to corporation tax.

Your accountant will advise you how to apportion your profits between salaries and retained profits to your best advantage. He or she will also be needed for drawing up the accounts because, although corporation tax returns are not particularly complicated, the Companies Act 1985 demands more advanced and complex accounting from a company than from a sole trader. This Act also requires that company accounts be audited by a suitably qualified accountant. Companies with a turnover of no more than £90,000 a year are exempt from this requirement. Companies with a turnover above that limit but less than £350,000 a year (and a balance sheet of no more than £1.4 million) will be allowed to submit a less rigorous report from an independent accountant.

Capital allowances and losses: limited companies

These are the same for companies as for sole traders and partnerships, but cannot be offset against the directors' or shareholders' income from other sources: they apply only to the company's income.

A trading loss in any one period may be offset, retrospectively, against the profits in the previous year. Or else the loss may be carried forward indefinitely to offset the profits of subsequent years from the same trade.

Accounting period: limited companies

A company may choose any date it likes for its accounting period. Corporation tax is, however, charged by reference to the fiscal financial year which runs from 1 April to 31 March and if (as is often the case) the company's accounting period is different, then the trading profits of two periods will be apportioned on a time basis. For instance, if a company has chosen January to December as its accounting period, then the apportionment will take 9/12 of trading profits of one period and 3/12 of the other one. Other income and any capital gains are not apportioned; the tax due is calculated on the basis of the accounting period within which they fall, rather than tax years.

Tax is due nine months from the end of the accounting period (that is, September in the case of a January to December accounting period).

Capital profits

Sole traders and partnerships, as well as limited companies, from time to time make capital profits: for example, on the sale of a business property or goodwill. Sole traders and partners may be liable to capital gains tax (CGT) on the capital profit; limited companies do not pay capital gains tax, but instead pay corporation tax on capital profit calculated in accordance with the capital gains tax regulations.

The calculations of any tax liability on the disposal of a business asset and of the reliefs available are very complex, and professional assistance from your accountant will almost certainly be necessary.

The main reliefs available against capital gains are as follows:

- *indexation allowance*: this deducts any gains due to inflation since March 1982. But indexation allowances may not be used to create or increase a capital loss
- *capital losses*: these can be set against gains
- *tax-free allowance*: individuals (e.g. sole traders) can make gains up to a given amount each year tax-free
- *roll-over relief*: if you dispose of 'qualifying' business assets you can defer CGT on any gain, providing you reinvest an amount equal to the disposal proceeds. You must reinvest in a new qualifying asset within three years after, or one year before, the disposal. Qualifying assets include land or property, goodwill and fixed plant or machinery.
- *reinvestment relief*: tax due on any gains made by individuals – but not companies – may be deferred if the proceeds are re-invested in the shares of an unquoted trading company, provided certain conditions are met
- *retirement relief*: where an individual disposes of a business or certain assets on retirement, the first £250,000 of any gain is tax-free together with half the next £750,000 of gain. This relief is scaled down if you have been running the business for less than ten years
- *hold-over relief*: if you give away business assets or shares in an unquoted company – e.g. by passing them on to younger members of your family – you may be able to defer any CGT that would otherwise be due.

Value Added Tax (VAT)

This is a tax normally payable quarterly, not to the Inland Revenue but to HM Customs and Excise, on the supply of most goods and services in Great Britain. It consists of input and output tax. There are three kinds of registration: compulsory, voluntary and intending.

The tax you pay on goods and services that you buy for your business is called input tax: the tax you charge your customers is called output tax. At present, the main rate for both is 17.5 per cent.

This is how it works: Bill buys raw materials for £235, inclusive of 17.5 per cent VAT; £35 is his input tax. He uses the materials to manufacture products selling for £450, before VAT. So the selling price would amount to £528.75 of which £78.75 is his output tax. He deducts the input tax from it, and remits the balance (£43.75) to Customs and Excise. If his input tax had been greater than his output tax, he would have been refunded the difference.

At present there are four categories of goods and services:

- *exempt*: on which no VAT is payable under any circumstances (for example, insurance, doctors' services)
- *zero-rated*: on which, in theory, tax is payable but, in practice, none is paid, because the tax rate is zero per cent (for example, some exported goods and food in shops)
- *standard-rated*: on which VAT at 17.5 per cent is charged. This applies to the majority of goods and services. The figure is liable to change at the Government's decision.
- *reduced-rated*: this applies only to domestic fuel and some energy-saving installations, on which VAT is currently charged at 5 per cent.

The difference between exempt and zero-rated may seem trivial, but is actually important. You cannot claim refunds of input tax unless you are collecting output tax, if only notionally. If you dealt only in exempt supplies, you would not be a 'taxable person', and could not be registered for VAT. You could not then recover any of the input tax you paid on your supplies, such as telephone charges and stationery, any more than a private person can.

However, this is not the case if you deal only in zero-rated supplies (for example, if you are an exporter). You can claim refunds of your input tax – unless you exercise a zero-rated option of trader's exemption from VAT, in which case you lose these refunds. Note that there are strict conditions to meet if you are exporting within the European Union (see Chapter 15).

Compulsory registration

You must register for VAT if, at the end of any month, your total taxable turnover exceeds £49,000 (from 1 December 1997) or if you have reasonable grounds for believing that your taxable turnover in the next 30 days will exceed £49,000. Trade in zero-rated supplies counts towards your turnover, but not trade in exempt supplies.

If you buy a going concern from a VAT-registered trader, you must be registered too – and may be allowed to go on using the same VAT registration number, although this should only be considered after careful discussion with your accountant or solicitor, since it would make you liable for amounts owed to Customs and Excise by the previous business. (If you decide VAT registration is not to your advantage, perhaps if you intend to run the business on a smaller scale, you can apply for deregistration.) You should get your registration in order before you sign the contract to buy the business. The leaflet *Transfer of a business as a going concern* (700/9) is available from your VAT office.

As soon as you know that you will have to register for VAT, contact your local VAT office, at Customs and Excise, which will send you forms to fill in. Once you have done this, you must immediately start charging your customers VAT and keeping records, without waiting to be allotted a registration number because you yourself will be charged VAT from the moment you become liable for registration. However, you must not show VAT as a separate item in your invoices until you have been allocated a VAT registration number. Include the amount of the tax in your prices, and tell your customers that you have done so. Then, within 30 days of getting your registration number, you must send out another set of invoices, showing VAT separately, to those of your customers who are themselves registered, and so will be claiming it back.

It is best not to get into arrears, which you may find it difficult to recover from your customers in retrospect. And it is worth setting up a system from the very beginning, because it is hard to do several months' books in arrears.

You must keep records of all transactions: do not make guesses. Keep for inspection all invoices you receive which show payment of VAT – you will not be allowed to reclaim the VAT without these. You have to make quarterly returns showing your input and output tax, and submit to having your VAT records inspected at intervals. There are civil penalties for defaulting on payments, or for failing to register for VAT on time.

VAT leaflet 700/1 *Should I Be Registered for VAT?* explains in detail the compulsory registration rules.

Voluntary registration

With a turnover under £49,000 a year, you may still apply for VAT registration if you are able to convince Customs and Excise that this is applicable to your business. Some of the advantages of registration include:

- You can claim back all your input tax (for instance, on equipment you have to buy when setting up). This is especially advantageous if your goods or services are zero-rated.
- If you start trading unregistered and your turnover grows to the point where you have to register, the addition of VAT will increase all your prices: this will dismay your customers, if they are consumers and not registered traders, and so cannot claim back the increase.
- VAT can ease your cash flow difficulties. If you arrange to make major purchases just before you are due to make out a return, your input VAT will be refunded shortly after you get the invoice, even though you may be receiving three months' credit from your suppliers. (But this scheme will work against you if you give credit to customers: you will have to pay your output VAT months before you get paid.)

Some of the disadvantages of registration are:

- The record-keeping and accounting demanded by VAT are an addition to your labours which you may not welcome if you employ a small number of staff, or none. Matters become still more complicated if you deal in a variety of goods, some standard-rated and others zero-rated: for example, stationery and books.

- If you are an exporter, you must be able to prove (by means of the relevant shipping documents) that your goods were, in fact, sold abroad. If some of your trade is in export and some is home trade, you will have the complication of selling goods differently rated.

If, having registered, you find that the disadvantages outweigh the advantages, you can cancel your registration, provided that your annual turnover is below £47,000 – leaflet 700/1 explains the rules.

Pre-registration expenses

You can claim back up to six months' input tax on purchases made before you registered for VAT, providing various conditions are met. And, if you are starting a business in the course of which you intend to produce 'taxable supplies' at some future date, but have not yet started to do so, you can apply for VAT registration beforehand. You will have to show convincing documentary evidence (such as contracts, licences, planning permission) of firm arrangements to make the taxable supplies. If this is accepted, you may be able to claim back some of the input tax you have paid, provided that it is wholly attributable to the intended production of taxable supplies.

Cash accounting scheme

This is open to all firms whose taxable turnover (excluding VAT) does not exceed £350,000. Under this scheme, VAT accounts are rendered, not on the basis of the tax invoices, but on the basis of money actually paid and received. This offers special advantages to businesses giving extended credit to customers – they need not account for VAT on credit transactions until they have received payment, and they enjoy automatic bad debt relief.

This scheme is not particularly advantageous, however, to traders, such as most retailers, who are paid in full at the time of the sale. You can also claim bad debt relief even if you are not in the cash accounting scheme.

Retail schemes

Customs and Excise provides a number of retail schemes for calculating VAT: these are intended for shopkeepers and other retail traders, for whom the system of issuing a tax invoice for each sale would be impracticable. There is a choice of retail schemes, of which one or more could be appropriate; consult your VAT office before deciding on any of them.

Annual accounting scheme

This is open to traders who have already been registered for at least one year, and whose annual taxable turnover (excluding VAT) does not exceed £300,000. It works like this: your VAT liability is estimated on the basis of the previous year's payments, and divided into ten monthly portions. Nine of these you pay by direct debit. You then have two months for sending in your annual VAT return, and making the tenth, balancing payment.

This system means that you have to make only one return a year, instead of four; and knowing in advance how much you are going to be paying, you are spared unpleasant jolts to your cash flow calculations. The balancing payment is less predictable, but you have an extra month's grace.

Businesses with a very low turnover (£100,000 a year or less) have a further option. You need make no interim payments if your previous year's net VAT liability was under £2,000. If it was over £2,000, you can make three quarterly payments of 20 per cent of the previous year's net VAT liability, and then a balancing payment.

Chapter 8

How to be an employer

Yes, there is such a thing as a one-man or one-woman business, particularly if what is being offered is a service or a consultancy. A plumber or electrician, for instance, needs only a mobile phone or telephone-answering machine to record customers' calls: he or she can call them back in the evenings, and do the bookkeeping on Sundays.

Many small firms start up with no other staff than the entrepreneur and his or her family, or a partner. But unless the family is large and willing, the firm will soon be needing some other employees, if it is to achieve progress.

In fact, a manufacturing business is likely to need employees from the start. It may only be a case of a couple of part-timers, or outworkers, or a clerical assistant; even so, the businessman or businesswoman immediately becomes an employer, and should find out how to go about it.

Finding and recruiting staff

When you have decided to take on employees, start by defining exactly what their duties are to be and what experience, skills and qualities are required to do the job. Avoid the temptation to ask for experience and qualifications greater than are necessary. This will make it easier for you to find the right person and easier, also, for any applicant to decide whether the job is the right one for him or her. A good working relationship is much more likely to develop if both you and your workers are suited to each other.

Ways of finding suitable employees include the Employment Service (listed in the telephone directory), employment agencies (which charge the employer a fee), personal recommendation or advertisements in your local, national or trade press or local radio stations.

If you have a shop or factory with an entrance on the main road, place an advertisement where it can be seen by passers-by. Or advertise for new workers by placing cards in local shops. This is cheap and generally produces a good response. Specify exactly what is wanted – and if you are willing to train new staff, make this clear.

It is sometimes easier and more economical to contract casual, part-time or freelance workers than employ full-time permanent staff, particularly when employing people with family commit-ments who are keen to get jobs which can be done partly at home, or with flexible hours, perhaps not coming in to work during school holidays.

It can be a bad mistake to employ acquaintances; this can prove embarrassing if they turn out to be no good. Also, do not try to recruit staff when you already have large orders and are very busy. This would be inefficient because it does not allow time for training.

Remember that any advertisement, wherever it is placed, must not exclude anyone on grounds of race, sex, marital status or dis-ability, except in a very few closely defined cases.

Your local Employment Service can provide a fast, free recruit-ment service for all types of jobs, and staff can advise on selection and can provide information on employment legislation. Ask whether you could benefit from any of the Government's special schemes for promoting employment. For example, the Work Trials scheme allows you to 'try out' a potential staff member for up to 15 days, without completing any DSS or Inland Revenue paperwork.

You may decide to employ young people and train them yourself. For workers aged under 18, you need to make a formal assessment of the risks arising from the work, giving a copy to the parent if the child is under 16. Consult your local careers service office about this and for advice on training. General information about training your staff (including small firm training awards and loans) is avail-able from Business Link.*

If you are looking for a worker with a particular skill which is in short supply locally, Employment Service offices can give a wide circulation to the vacancy, to attract workers from other areas.

Workers with particular skills may already be employed elsewhere and you may need to offer them terms that are in some way an improvement on what they are getting or can get in their present jobs. If a worker is at present employed locally, make sure his or her existing contract of employment does not prohibit him or her from leaving to take up a similar job within, say, five miles of the existing workplace, otherwise both of you could end up with a costly court case.

If you ask for references, be sure to take them up, preferably in writing. You should also check that your employees are not working illegally – you risk prosecution if, as an employer, you breach the Asylum and Immigration Act 1996. Acceptable checks include seeing a P45, P60 or payslip showing a National Insurance number: the Home Office Employers' HelpLine★ can give further information.

Paying wages and salaries

You do not have a free hand in negotiating pay with your employees. Quite apart from the normal constraints of the 'going rate' for the job, a national minimum wage is planned to come into effect some time in 1999. The minimum wage will apply in all regions, business sectors and sizes of firms, with very few exceptions (the 'genuinely self-employed' being one). Workers will have the right to go to an industrial tribunal or county court to recover the difference if they have been paid less than the national minimum wage.

At the time of writing, a commission was carrying out work to establish the initial level at which the minimum wage should be set, but other issues are also still to be decided: for example, what constitutes 'pay', and the age at which it should apply (there will be 'special rules' for workers under 26).

Another factor affecting wage levels may be an agreement between the employers' federation of your trade and the appropriate trade unions, which may be binding on you. If there are similar businesses in the area, it is wise to find out what they are paying, and if it is related to a union rate. Men and women doing the same or broadly similar work are, of course, entitled to the same rates of pay.

When it comes to paying your employees, your accountant will tell you how to set up a wages book, and may agree, for a fee, to look after your payroll until you are sufficiently organised to take care of it yourself.

Avoiding employment disputes

The independent Advisory, Conciliation and Arbitration Service (ACAS)* can be consulted on matters relating to employment and industrial relations. Though this organisation is mostly known to the public as a conciliator in industrial disputes or disputes between individuals and their employers, a considerable part of its work is preventive and consists of advising both sides of industry on industrial relations matters, including finding their way through the complications of employment legislation.

The ACAS head office is in London. Offices in Scotland, Wales and in English regions deal with written and telephone enquiries. Their addresses and telephone numbers can be found in local telephone directories. Visits to employers' premises by ACAS advisers can be arranged, and booklets are available about recruitment and selection, workplace communications, job evaluation, discipline at work, and other aspects of employment.

Rights of employees

It is important for new entrepreneurs to understand the rights of employees under current legislation. A useful summary is the free DTI leaflet, *Employing Staff*, available from DTI Small Firms Publications.*

Fuller information is available in the ACAS booklet, entitled *Employing People*, written specially for small firms; it contains straightforward guidance on a wide range of employment matters, from hiring people and employment contracts, to absence, labour turnover and unfair dismissal. It costs £2 plus £1 postage and packing, from ACAS Reader Ltd.* In addition, the Department of Trade and Industry publishes material on employment legislation which covers every topic that you should be informed about. You can get copies from your local Employment Service office or from DTI Small Firms Publications* (leaflet reference numbers are given after each of the headings below). Only a brief outline can be given here.

Some of the rights below, such as statutory maternity pay, apply only to employees who have worked for you for a minimum period. Note, though, that part-time employees have the same rights as full-timers.

Written statement of employment terms (URN 96/1015)

You must give every employee who is employed for at least a month a written statement setting out the conditions and terms on which he or she is employed (sometimes called a 'contract of employment', though that is not strictly correct: the contract was formed earlier, when you made someone a firm offer of a job and it was firmly accepted).

The contract is legally enforceable as soon as an employee starts work. Note that not everything has to be in writing to become part of the contract. For example, all employment contracts are taken to require that you and your employee should act in good faith towards each other. And other unwritten conditions can become part of the contract 'by custom and practice', if they are reasonable and generally applied in your area or trade for some time.

The written statement must be given within two months of starting work and contain information on at least the following:

- name of the employer and employee
- date of starting employment (and, possibly, the start date for employment with the previous employer if it counts as part of one continuous period of employment)
- title of job or description of employee's job
- rates of pay (including any overtime) and how they are calculated
- whether payment is to be by cheque, cash or bank transfer
- when payment is to be made (weekly or monthly)
- hours of work (regular and overtime, if applicable)
- holidays and holiday pay
- sick pay arrangements
- pension scheme arrangements
- length of notice required from employer and from employee
- rules relating to disciplinary procedures
- length of employment and end date – if not permanent
- place of work
- collective agreements
- rules relating to requirements to work outside the UK.

If any of these points does not apply, for instance if there are no pension arrangements, the document must say so explicitly.

It is the practice of many employers to confirm an oral offer of a job by letter, setting out the conditions and terms. If all these above points are covered, such a letter will do in place of a written statement; if they are not, a written statement will still be necessary.

The terms set out in the statement can only rarely be altered without the consent of both parties. If you transfer the employee to another kind of work or promote him or her, you may need to provide a new written statement.

Itemised pay statement (URN 96/1012)

With each wage payment, you must give each employee a wage slip showing gross pay, deductions (with the reason given for each, such as income tax, National Insurance contributions, union dues) and the net pay.

You will, of course, need to keep a copy of this for your own records. If you pay wages in cash, get your copy signed by the employee, as a receipt.

Suspending employees from work (URN 96/1014)

If business is bad, you may want to put some employees on short time, or even lay them off without pay, or with pay at a lower rate. Your right to do so should be specified at the time of engaging an employee. You should also be aware that most employees are entitled to a guaranteed payment for up to five working days in any three months in which you have no work for them to do.

Continuous employment (PL711)

Many employees' rights depend on their being continuously employed. Some breaks in employment, such as maternity leave, do not break continuity; others, no matter how short, do. The full rules are explained in the leaflet.

Time off work (URN 96/1013)

You should allow time off to employees engaged on some trade union or public duties: for example, justices of the peace, local councillors, school governors. A pregnant employee also has the right to time off for visits to antenatal clinics and employees are allowed time off for job-hunting or training if you are making them redundant. Time off should be with pay, unless it is for public duties or some trade union activities.

Maternity rights (URN 96/1011)

Where an employee is stopping work to have a baby, you will have to pay her statutory maternity pay (SMP) if:

- she has been working for you continuously for at least 26 weeks ending with the 15th week before the baby is due (this 15th week is known as the qualifying week)
- she has average weekly earnings of not less than the current lower earnings limit for the payment of National Insurance contributions
- she must still be pregnant in the 11th week before the expected week of confinement, or must have already given birth (there are special regulations for premature births)
- she has actually stopped work
- she has given you proper advance notice of her intentions.

A woman fulfilling these conditions can get SMP for up to 18 weeks starting not earlier than the 11th week before the expected date of confinement. As a 'small employer' (paying £20,000 a year or less in gross National Insurance contributions), you may deduct the gross amount of the SMP from the total sum of National Insurance contributions (your own and your staff's) which you have to pay, plus 6.5 per cent compensation. Larger employees may reclaim only 92 per cent of the SMP payments.

All pregnant employees, however short their service with you, have a right to 14 weeks' maternity leave (longer in a few cases), during which they retain all their normal terms and conditions of employment (except pay). At the end of her leave, an employee is entitled to come back to work for you in her former job or, if that post becomes redundant, a suitable alternative if there is one.

A woman who has worked for you for at least two years by the beginning of the 11th week before her baby is due is entitled to a longer maternity absence – up to the end of the 28th week after the week in which her child is born. However, her normal terms and conditions of employment do not automatically apply – it depends on her contract of employment, or, if that is silent on the matter, negotiation between you. And to take advantage of her rights, your employee must also comply with various notification rules. She must tell you of her intention to return to work (in writing, at least 21 days before her absence begins) and must produce a certificate

(MatB1) of expected confinement, if you want to see it. Not earlier than 21 days before the end of her maternity leave, you may write to her to ask her if she still intends to return, and she must reply within 14 days. She must also let you know the date on which she wants to return, at least 21 days in advance.

If you have no more than five employees when a woman starts her maternity leave, you may not have to keep her job open for her, but if you do not, you should be very sure that you are not guilty of sex discrimination.

When employees fall ill

Under the statutory sick pay scheme (SSP), an employer must pay employees sick pay for up to 28 weeks' illness. Spells of illness shorter than four days (including Saturdays, Sundays and holidays) do not qualify for sick pay. The 28-week maximum 'period of inca-pacity for work' is not limited to one tax year: it may be made up of intermittent periods of illness, provided that the gap between any of these is not more than eight weeks. When an employee's illness, whether 'linked' or continuous, lasts longer than 28 weeks, your obligation ceases and state benefit takes over; but your obligation starts again if, having recovered, the employee should fall ill again more than eight weeks after the end of a maximum period.

If you have a high proportion of your workforce sick at any one time you might be able to reclaim some of the SSP under the Percentage Threshold Scheme. Under the scheme you compare the SSP you have paid in one month with the total of your employers' and employees' Class 1 National Insurance contributions for that month. You can claim back any SSP over and above 13 per cent of your National Insurance liability.

For a detailed explanation of these rules, and also those of mater-nity entitlements, consult the booklets CA30 *SSP Manual for Employers* and CA29 *SMP Manual for Employers* available from your Benefits Agency office.

There is a government Employers' HelpLine,★ which, among other things, gives free telephone advice to employers about statutory sick pay, statutory maternity pay, and National Insurance contribu-tions. This service is intended to be particularly helpful to new or established small businesses without a separate wages department.

Disciplinary procedures

Disciplinary procedures can help to ensure that disciplinary offences are dealt with fairly and consistently, as well as minimising disagreements about disciplinary matters and reducing the need for dismissals. This may be particularly important if an employee should complain to an industrial tribunal of unfair dismissal, since the employer will need to show the tribunal that the dismissal was fair.

The ACAS advisory handbook *Discipline at Work* contains comprehensive practical advice on handling disciplinary matters, and gives examples of rules, and of a disciplinary procedure, for a small company – contact ACAS Reader Ltd.★ In addition, ACAS has a code of practice, *Disciplinary Practice and Procedures in Employment*.

Disciplinary rules

Clear rules benefit both employer and employees, set standards of conduct at work, and make clear to employees what is expected of them. Employees will more readily accept rules if care is taken to explain why they are necessary. Rules should cover such matters as timekeeping; absence; health and safety; use of company telephones, equipment and other facilities; and race and sex discrimination.

The rules should also specify the kind of offences that will be regarded as gross misconduct, and which could lead to dismissal without notice. Serious offences such as physical violence, theft or fraud are normally so regarded, but the nature of the business or other circumstances may determine that other offences should also be included.

The ACAS code of practice

The ACAS Code states that disciplinary procedures should:

- be in writing
- specify to whom they apply
- provide for matters to be dealt with quickly
- indicate the disciplinary actions which may be taken
- specify the levels of management which have the authority to take the various forms of disciplinary action, ensuring that immediate superiors do not normally have the power to dismiss without reference to senior management

- provide for individuals to be informed of the complaints against them, and to be given an opportunity to state their case before decisions are reached
- give individuals the right to be accompanied by a trade union representative, or by a fellow employee of their choice when stating their case
- ensure that, except for gross misconduct, no employees are dismissed for a first breach of discipline
- ensure that disciplinary action is not taken until the case has been carefully investigated
- ensure that individuals are given an explanation for any penalty imposed
- provide a right of appeal and specify the procedure to be followed.

In addition, disciplinary procedures should:

- apply to all employees, irrespective of their length of service
- be non-discriminatory
- ensure that any investigatory period of suspension is with pay, and specify how pay is to be calculated during such a period (if, exceptionally, suspension is to be without pay, this should be provided for in the contract of employment)
- ensure that, where the facts are in dispute, no disciplinary penalty is imposed until the case has been carefully investigated and it has been concluded, on the balance of probability, that the employee committed the act in question.

Disciplinary penalties

Informal action, such as counselling, should generally precede formal warnings. If an informal approach fails, then formal penalties are normally implemented progressively. There are typically four stages:

- oral warning
- first written warning
- final written warning
- dismissal.

While there are normally three stages before dismissal, they may be dispensed with if the employee's alleged misconduct warrants such action.

Rights to notice (PL707)

An employee who has worked for you for one month or more is entitled to a week's notice or a week's salary in lieu of notice, unless the contract of employment specified a longer period of notice. After two years, one week's notice is required for each year of working for you, up to a maximum of 12 weeks. Every employee is entitled to a written statement of the reason for being dismissed, if he or she asks for one.

Industrial tribunal

A dismissed employee may bring a complaint of unfair dismissal to an industrial tribunal only after a minimum of two years' continuous employment. However, there is no qualifying period for employees who allege that they were dismissed because of trade union activity, or for non-membership of a union, because of sex or race discrimination, pregnancy or childbirth, or because they asserted their entitlement to one of the legal rights described earlier in the chapter.

The industrial tribunal will take account of the firm's size and resources when deciding whether a dismissal was fair or not, and whether to direct re-employment. For instance, if a worker has proved not up to the physical demands of the job, a small firm may not have another job to offer, and may therefore dismiss the employee.

Employees (or applicants) who feel that they have been unlawfully treated under the Disability Discrimination Act 1995 (see page 138) can also complain to an industrial tribunal.

Note that at the time of writing new legislation was going through Parliament to introduce, as an alternative to industrial tribunals, an ACAS arbitration scheme. This legislation will also change the name of the tribunals to employment tribunals.

Consult *Dismissal: Fair or Unfair* (URN 96/1009), available from DTI Small Firms Publications.★

Making employees redundant

Employees may have to be made redundant when a firm is not doing enough business to justify their employment. A redundancy dismissal can be unfair on the basis of improper selection, lack of consultation and lack of notice. It should certainly not be motivated by personal reasons. A worker who thinks you are making him or her redundant just to get rid of him or her can challenge your decision before an industrial tribunal.

Redundancy pay is due to those employees who have at least two years' continuous service. Service before the age of 18 does not count. See *Redundancy Payments* (PL808), available from the Redundancy Payments Service,* which also operates a free helpline (and supplies the other two leaflets in this section).

There is an obligation on the employer to inform the Department of Trade and Industry if he or she is going to make 20 or more people redundant. You can get a form on which to do so from your local Employment Services office. Look also at *Redundancy Consultation and Notification* (PL833).

If the employees are members of a trade union, there is an obligation for the employer to consult with the trade union at the 'earliest opportunity'. When 10 to 99 redundancies are proposed within a 30-day period, then the employers are required to enter into at least 30 days' consultation with the trade union before the first dismissal takes place.

One important point to be aware of if you take over a going concern, is that workers' employment is deemed in law to be continuing. So if you decide to replace some of them, you may find yourself with a good deal of compensation to pay, even though you did not hire these people, and they have not worked for you for very long. This is one of the dangers of taking over a going concern, so before you do so, ask for a roll of employees, showing their length of continuous employment there, so that you can assess the amount of possible redundancy pay.

Look also at *Employment Rights on the Transfer of an Undertaking* (PL699). If you know in advance that you will want to make employees redundant, negotiate with the seller of the business about which of you is to pay.

Avoiding discrimination

Employees have the right to belong (or not to belong) to a trade union. If any of your employees are members of a trade union, you will do well to read *Trade Union Membership* (URN 96/1010) from

DTI Small Firms Publications.★ Note also that a trade union official may have a legal right to paid time off for his or her duties.

You should also be aware that there are laws concerning sex, race and disability discrimination in employment. The Equal Opportunities Commission★ publishes leaflets and booklets on sex discrimination; for information on the Race Relations Act contact the Commission for Racial Equality.★

The employment provisions of the Disability Discrimination Act 1995 (DDA) apply if you have 20 or more employees. Broadly, the effect is that an employee with a disability must not be less favourably treated for a reason related to their disability than other people, without justification. Employers may also have to make 'reasonable adjustments' if their premises or working arrangements place an employee with a disability at a substantial disadvantage. The Act does not prevent you from hiring the best person for the job – its aim is to ensure that someone with a disability, who could be that best person, is considered fairly. A booklet, *Discrimination Act 1995 – What employers need to know*, is available from the DDA information line.★

A one-day course on employment law is among the courses organised by the Industrial Society.★

Health and safety of employees

The responsibilities concerning the health, safety and welfare of people at work are defined in broad terms by the Health and Safety at Work Act 1974. It places important general duties on all people at work – employers, employees and the self-employed, manufacturers, suppliers, designers and importers of materials used at work, and people in control of premises. More detailed and specific requirements are laid down by the Workplace (Health, Safety and Welfare) Regulations 1992 which specify what must be provided in the way of washrooms, lavatories, heat, ventilation and light, somewhere to sit, and so on. Other regulations and codes of practice apply to many different work activities.

The requirements to protect health and safety and provide welfare vary considerably depending on the type of work being carried on. You need to assess how risky your business is (and must keep a written risk assessment if you employ five or more people). You should also establish what facilities and safeguards you must provide in matters such as machinery guards, protective clothing, storage and handling of dangerous substances.

The first step is to register with the appropriate enforcing authority, which may visit to inspect your premises. For most shops, offices, warehouses, leisure facilities, hotel and catering activities, the enforcing authority is the local authority. In the case of manufacturing and most other businesses, it is the Health and Safety Executive (HSE).

Addresses of local authority enforcement offices can be obtained from district council offices or, in case of difficulty, from the local authority liaison officer in the nearest HSE area office. There are some 20 such offices, and a Health and Safety Executive InfoLine.*

The HSE publishes a range of explanatory and guidance material; some publications are available free of charge from HSE offices. The booklet, *Essentials of Health and Safety at Work*, is obtainable from HSE Books* or from bookshops. The HSE produces a list of all its publications, and this can be obtained free of charge by contacting the InfoLine. There are also free subject catalogues covering topics such as agriculture, asbestos and construction work.

All accidents at work, whether they involve employees or visitors to your premises, must be recorded, and all serious ones, including those which lead to having three or more days off or at least one day in hospital, must be reported on a special form to the relevant enforcing authority. Near-miss accidents must also be reported. Every place of work should have a well-equipped first-aid box (equipped according to the number of employees on site and the nature of the work), the contents of which are specified. The employees should know where it is kept and there should be a correct ratio of trained first-aiders to staff (in offices it is 1:50). All businesses, however small, must appoint someone to take control of accidents and look after the first-aid box.

PAYE

You are the channel by which your employees' Pay As You Earn (PAYE) income tax is transmitted to the Board of Inland Revenue, as well as their National Insurance contributions (and yours too).

Leaflet CWL3, *Thinking of Taking Someone On?*, obtainable from tax offices, explains and clearly illustrates the procedure. If you employ anyone in your business in return for wages, even members of your own family, you are responsible for deducting their income tax and National Insurance at source and sending it to the Inland Revenue. (As a small employer you can pay quarterly rather than monthly.) As soon as you hire someone, let your tax office know, using form CWF3, which is included in the leaflet above: you will be told which is to be your PAYE office. You will then be told what your employee's PAYE reference number will be, and shortly after that you will receive a copy of the 'New Employer's Starter Pack'. Included in the pack is a copy of the *Employer's Quick Guide to PAYE and NICs*, which covers the main points of the system.

An employee who has previously been employed and paid tax should bring you his or her P45 form which has on it a code number and total pay and total tax to date in the financial year. A new employee without a P45 should be asked to sign a form P46 (in your New Employer's Starter Pack) which you then complete and send to your PAYE office. Until you hear from their tax office again, you work out their tax using an 'emergency code'.

The New Employer's Starter Pack contains two sets of printed tables. By looking up each employee's code number in the tables, you will know how much tax to deduct each week or month. You enter the amount, the gross salary and other details on each employee's deductions working sheet, which has a space for each week of the tax year. At regular intervals you must send the deducted tax and insurance contributions to the tax Accounts Office.

At the end of the tax year, all the information concerning each employee's wages, income tax and National Insurance contributions must be entered on a form P14. A copy is sent to the PAYE tax district, together with form P35, which is an annual statement. Another copy (certificate P60) goes to the employee.

National Insurance

As an employer, you are also responsible for collecting all your employees' National Insurance contributions every week or month, together with their income tax, and sending them on to the

Inland Revenue together with yours, the employer's contributions. You work out the contributions from tables supplied in the New Employer's Starter Pack.

Arrangements exist for employees to contract out of part of their contributions where a firm has an occupational pension scheme, but this is unlikely to concern you at this stage.

You will be concerned with three kinds of contributions, as listed in the table overleaf.

Class 1 contributions

These are due from each of your employees who is 16 or over and below the minimum state pension age (currently 65 for a man, 60 for a woman) whose earnings reach the lower earnings limit. For each of them, you must pay the employer's share. (Contributions are not due from employees over state pension age, but you must continue to pay the employer's share.) Obviously the lower earnings limit figure is one to bear in mind when employing part-time staff. If you go over this limit, both the employee and you have to pay National Insurance contributions, and an apparently generous pay increase may prove a lot less lavish after extra deductions for National Insurance and tax.

Note that if you take on someone who has been unemployed for two years or more, or a trainee on certain Government schemes, you will have no National Insurance to pay on their wages for up to a year.

If yours is a limited company, you as an individual pay an employee's share, and the company pays an employer's contribution – although, in effect, in a small company you would be paying both the sums.

Class 2 contributions

You pay these if you are a sole trader or a partner, but there are some state benefits to which they do not entitle you, notably unemployment benefit. You pay either by quarterly bills or monthly direct debit. You can claim exemption from Class 2 payments if you are able to show that your net earnings from self-employment in a tax year are expected to be below a certain sum (£3,590 from 6 April 1998). You must apply to the Department of Social Security for a certificate of exemption in advance.

National Insurance contributions (as from April 1998)

Type of contri-bution	Category of insured person	Basis of contri-bution	Earnings limit lower	upper	Amount paid
Class 1	employed earners	earnings-related	£64 a week	£485 a week (employees only)	*employee:* nil if earnings less than £64; otherwise, 2% on first £64 and 10% on the rest up to £485 *employer:* nil if earnings less than £64; above £64, on sliding scale ranging from 3% for weekly earnings below £110, up to 10% for earnings over £210
Class 2	self-employed	flat rate	–	–	£6.35 a week
Class 4	self-employed	earnings-related	£7,310 annual profits	£25,220	6% of amount by which profits exceed lower earnings limit, up to £25,220

Class 4 contributions

These are payable by Class 2 payers whose taxable profits exceed a certain sum; there is an upper limit on the amount payable (see the Table opposite).

Class 4 contributions are assessed together with income tax by the Inland Revenue and are collected at the same time as your income tax.

If you start your business in your spare time while continuing to work for an employer, you must pay all three types of contribution – Class 1, Class 2 and Class 4. There is, however, an upper limit, and anything you pay over this amount in a tax year will be refunded to you.

For more detailed information about National Insurance, go direct to the source, the Contributions Agency (in your phone book). Leaflets and information are available by phoning the government Employers' Helpline.*

Chapter 9

Insurance for the small business

When you are just starting up in business and every penny counts, having to pay insurance premiums can seem to be an uncalled-for imposition. But you would see this in a different light if the occasion arose to put in a claim. Then you might start to worry whether you had taken enough insurance to cover all the losses you had suffered.

Almost every aspect of trading can create a need for some kind of insurance. For most kinds you can find cover, but sometimes the premiums may be high. However, the premiums paid for any business insurance are deductible expenses which can be set off against tax.

Employer's liability insurance

The law currently requires that everyone on your payroll (except for members of your family and domestic servants) must be covered by this insurance, and that a current certificate of insurance be displayed at the place of work. However, there are proposals to exempt the very smallest firms from the requirement.

The employer's liability insurance covers you for claims that might arise if an employee suffered physical injury or illness in the course of, or resulting from, his or her employment. It would be necessary for the employee suing you for damages to show that the injury or illness arose not from his or her own inadvertence, but from your negligence or that of another employee.

You would be wise to include employed members of the family in the insurance cover, even though you do not need to. Close relationship does not preclude a claim for damages, and if one of your nearest and dearest were to suffer, you would be glad to have him or her compensated by the insurance company.

Most insurance companies will quote you rates for this type of insurance. The premiums are related to the size of your payroll and will also depend on the risks attached to the jobs. If your employees do office work only, it is likely to cost less than if they work with machinery or shift heavy loads.

The Health and Safety Executive Infoline★ publishes a free brochure, *Employer's Liability Guide* (HSE 4).

Insuring business property and equipment

You would be foolhardy not to insure for the various disasters that could mean the rapid end of your business, such as burglary, fire, flood, subsidence, malicious damage, explosion, to name but a few. Some of the features of a business that should be covered are:

- the business premises (including site clearance and rebuilding costs)
- the contents (including fixtures and fittings, industrial plant, computers, tools and other equipment)
- the stock (including supplies not yet used and goods that have been allocated to customers, even if the customer has not yet paid for them)
- goods in transit (on the way to the customer, or to a sub-contractor, or to the docks for shipment; in your own or someone else's vehicles; sent by post)
- goods on a sub-contractor's premises.

You could take out a separate policy for each kind of risk, but it would be more efficient to have a single insurance policy covering all risks.

Many trade associations arrange (or act as agents for) special insurance policies tailored for the needs of the particular trade.

The insurance should be revised and updated at regular intervals, otherwise you might find a huge discrepancy between the amount you are covered for and what your loss actually amounts to, should you need to make a claim.

Consequential loss insurance

This is a corollary to insuring against damage or theft: it covers further losses which would arise if your business were to come to a standstill following a disaster that is covered by the insurance.

Should your premises burn down, for instance, you would not only need to rebuild and re-equip but would also have to pay your wage bill and some overheads costs while no money was coming in. You might have lost all your stock and your office records and files, and by the time you were back in business, your customers might have gone elsewhere.

Consequential loss insurance should cover all these situations, loss of profit, and your overheads costs for a limited period.

Public liability insurance

Apart from the statutory insurance for liability to employees, there is insurance to cover you for claims by members of the public who have been injured as a result of your (or one of your employees') activities at work: for example, a brick dropped from scaffolding on passers-by.

Working from home

Your existing household insurance may cover your equipment and public liability if you work from home in a small way. But you must tell your insurer that you work from home, or you could find that your cover is invalid. Your insurer is also likely to insist on a special policy once your business equipment rises above a certain value, if your work involves people visiting your home, or if the risk of fire or theft is increased (because you store flammable materials, for example). Several companies now offer policies specially for people who work at home.

Product liability insurance

This covers you for claims arising out of faults in something you or your employees have designed, manufactured or serviced – if your folding chair collapses under a purchaser, say, or the washing-machine you have repaired gives a severe electrical shock. You may be held liable even if you have not been negligent

Another type of insurance – professional indemnity insurance – covers professionals or other people who provide a service against liability claims resulting from negligent work.

Insurance for car and driver

Third-party insurance is, of course, compulsory on all the firm's vehicles; and you should insure at the same time for theft and accidents, etc. If your vehicles are going to be driven by various persons, make sure yours is an all-drivers policy.

If your work involves a great deal of driving, you would be wise to insure for loss of your driving licence, which could otherwise mean the loss of your livelihood. The insurance cannot restore your licence, but it can supply the means to hire a chauffeur.

Insurance if money is lost

A policy of this sort can be bought either as a stand-alone policy or as part of a general business contents policy. It will cover you for loss of money (including cheques and postal orders) from your office, your till, from your house, or in transit – for instance, you could be robbed while taking it to the bank. Insurance can also be taken out to compensate an employee who is injured while being robbed of money.

Firms which hold clients' money, such as travel agents or insurance agents, need an insurance bond to protect them against loss if the business fails. Bonding is compulsory for some types of agency.

Other insurance

There is hardly a calamity for which you cannot insure your business or yourself. For instance, if you have a shop, you might enquire about a plate glass insurance policy, which would provide such facilities as having your broken window and/or door boarded up, speedy replacement of the glass, compensation for damage or injury by shattered glass, consequential loss of profits.

By becoming a member of the Federation of Small Businesses,★ you are automatically entitled to legal and professional expenses insurance of up to £50,000 for each claim. This gives you some financial protection for various problems which include Inland Revenue investigations, property disputes, jury service, personal injury and employment disputes, as well as a 24-hour telephone legal advice service. There is also an FSB insurance service should you want to buy other types of business insurance.

Individual membership costs £60 a year (plus a joining fee of £20), and includes a bi-monthly magazine.

Personal insurance

You should not neglect your own insurance needs. Any illness or accident which takes you out of circulation for any length of time could be damaging – or fatal – to your prospects.

If you have dependants, adequate life insurance is probably your first priority. However, permanent health insurance comes a very close second. This provides a regular income to compensate for your loss of income while you are unable to work through incapacity. You might also consider other forms of health insurance. Private medical insurance, for example, would give you some control over the timing of an operation, so that you could hasten treatment or organise it to coincide with a slack business period. Critical illness insurance pays out on the diagnosis of various critical illnesses, such as heart disease or cancer.

You should also consider insuring any key partner or employee without whom the business would suffer. 'Key person' insurance pays out to the business if the key person is out of action. You can organise life insurance, permanent health insurance or critical illness insurance on this basis. It is also possible to buy insurance in case you or another key person are called for jury service.

Another consideration is what would happen if anyone with a financial stake in the business, such as a partner or shareholder, were to die. There could be problems if their inheritors decided to sell their stake. Again, life insurance can provide the money for you to buy them out.

Pensions

Retirement may seem a distant prospect when you are starting up, but do not delay too long before sorting out a pension. The longer you wait, the larger your contributions will need to be if you are to retire on an acceptable income. Many self-employed people count on selling their business on retirement to produce a retirement income. Quite apart from the risk that you may not be able, or want, to do so, pensions carry generous tax incentives: contributions (within limits) are tax-free and the money grows in a (largely) tax-free fund.

If you are a sole trader or partner, you can buy a personal pension plan. This is simply a way of making your own pension arrangements by saving with a pension provider such as an insurance company. The plan provider invests your money to build up a cash fund. At a set retirement date (which need not be when you actually stop work) the money is used to provide a pension. Part of the fund can be taken as a tax-free lump sum.

If your business is set up as a company, you have more choice. You can set up your own employer pension scheme, but in practice your choice is likely to be between a personal pension plan, executive pension plan or small self-administered scheme.

Executive pension plans are special pension schemes designed for a small number of members. They are bound by the same rules as employer schemes, but in your role as employer you can pay large amounts into a plan, whereas the limits on personal pension plan contributions are more stringent. On the other hand, there is no limit to the overall benefits from a personal pension plan: benefits from an executive plan are limited.

Small self-administered schemes (SSASs) are small employer schemes, usually with fewer than 12 members. They can be a good choice for family-run companies since, although they are administered by specialists such as insurance companies, you have a wide choice about who will manage your money and how it will be invested. You can even, in some cases, invest in your own business (although this has been increasingly restricted in recent years). But this extra choice requires an extra tier of management charges and makes these schemes unrealistic unless around £100,000 or more is available to invest.

Your choice will be governed by the limits set by the Inland Revenue on how much you can contribute, the benefits you can draw, the flexibility of the scheme and how the money can be invested.

If it is the thought of committing yourself to long-term saving that deters you, remember that you have considerable scope for varying contributions in line with fluctuating profits in order to help you keep your tax bill to a minimum. You can buy single-premium personal pension plans instead of paying regular contributions (single premiums also tend to incur lower charges) and vary your contributions to executive schemes or SSASs. With personal pension plans, you can also use up unused tax relief from previous years (within limits).

Buying insurance

A useful introduction is the free booklet *Insurance Advice for Small Businesses*, available from the Association of British Insurers.★ Buying business insurance is complex and rather specialised, so there is a case for getting the advice of an insurance broker specialising in commercial insurance, particularly if you need some unusual type of insurance or if you are faced with what seem excessively high premium demands.

To find a good insurance broker, personal recommendation is likely to be best. Ask if insurance advisers are registered with the Insurance Brokers Registration Council★ (which they must be to call themselves 'brokers'). This is no guarantee of good service, but registered brokers do have to comply with various requirements.

To give advice on life insurance and pensions, advisers must comply with further regulations and be properly authorised either by a regulatory organisation such as the Personal Investment Authority★ or Financial Services Authority, or by one of a number of recognised professional bodies (which includes the Insurance Brokers Registration Council). You can check that someone is properly authorised by phoning the Financial Services Authority.★ However, again there are degrees of specialisation and it is wise to check what experience and expertise a company has for small businesses.

Insurance advisers are normally paid commission by the companies whose products they sell, but for pensions advice in particular it might be worth paying a fee to a specialist. The Society of Pension Consultants★ and the Association of Consulting Actuaries★ can both supply lists of members.

Chapter 10

Buying a computer

The justification for getting a computer is to increase the efficiency of your business at least enough to offset the cost of installing and running the computer.

To assess your needs, start by making a list of all the areas in which a computer could be used in your business: for example, standard letters and circulars, costings, estimates and quotations, bookkeeping and preparation of accounts, invoices and statements, financial projections (including forecasting of cash flow and profit and loss), stock control, payrolls (including PAYE and National Insurance).

If you consider that a lot of your office work falls within these areas, give serious consideration to buying a computer. A computer will be of assistance to almost any business, and is likely very quickly to justify itself either in financial terms or – perhaps equally importantly – in terms of saving your time.

Finding out about computers

Take your time in choosing a computer system. It is very important for you to acquire a system which does what you need it to do and which you find reasonably straightforward to operate. If you feel you are never going to come to grips with modern technology, then you should either steel yourself to go on an introductory course in the hope that it will cure you of any phobias, or else leave the subject alone; you may however have a partner or a member of staff to whom the detailed investigation of the subject can be delegated. But, in any event, you are going to need a rudimentary understanding of the subject. The truth is that a computer must be treated as a slave rather than a master, moreover as a rather stupid slave which is only going to perform correctly if its master accustoms himself to giving it unambiguous instructions which he knows to be within its competence.

The individual investigating the possible purchase of a computer has the choice of calling in a computer consultant at the very start, or else of first learning something about the subject and then of taking more expert advice. The size of your business will determine the appropriate approach.

A larger business will be more likely to need, and to be able to justify the cost of employing, a computer consultant whose charges will be of the order of £60 to £100 per hour. Try to make sure you obtain the services of a reputable consultant. The consultant will need to know how your business works: while this is no doubt obvious to you, you may find it another matter to analyse it with sufficient clarity for an outsider to understand fully. If he or she considers that it is viable for your business to invest in a computer, advice will be given on appropriate systems.

A smaller business will almost certainly start by carrying out its own initial investigations. You (or, if appropriate, your partner or appointed investigator) need to understand the type of work that computers do, and also the computer market generally.

Sources of information include:

- friends who work with computers
- other small businesses which are computerised
- computer courses: these range from brief introductory courses, some no longer than a day, to advanced subjects. They are advertised in computer and business magazines. Your local university or college or adult education centre may also run classes
- computer books: there are many on the market; make sure that what you buy is at the appropriate level of expertise for you
- computer exhibitions, of which there are surprisingly many
- computer and business magazines: again there are many of these and you should be able to find one or more at your level
- specialist shops (not the chain stores which sell computers – they tend to aim for the home computer market and are unlikely to offer more than a rudimentary expertise). Specialist shops usually sell a fairly limited range of hardware and software, and thus cannot be completely unbiased, but they tend to have a thorough knowledge of what they do sell

- the National Computing Centre★ (membership costs £495 a year excluding VAT)
- the Federation of Information Systems Centres, an independent government-established body, with centres located throughout the UK. Details from Systems Information Technology Group.★

What you need and the cost of buying it

The cost of a business computer starts at about £500; but the sky is the limit. In practice, you will probably find yourself spending about £1,000 on a reasonably up-to-date design giving substantial internal storage space for programs and information. However, the computer is only the first (albeit the most important) building block. In order to process and reproduce the information which you feed in, you must also buy:

- the program or programs which you intend to run on the computer – these are known as 'software' or 'applications'
- a printer (from £150)
- stationery and consumables – e.g. floppy disks, backup tapes, paper and other printer supplies
- a maintenance contract – you need to know that if your computer breaks down it will be repaired as soon as possible, and, preferably, that a replacement can be made available until your machine is back in running order. Some programs come provided with a maintenance contract. This provides for the producer to resolve any 'bugs' or other problems encountered, and sometimes also to supply the customer with any updates to the program. Such a contract may cost (per annum) up to 15 per cent of the cost of the computer or software to which it relates. Call-out fees for the engineers are often charged in addition, in which case what you have bought with your maintenance contract is little more than the availability of specialised help. However, without it you might be in dire straits. Many new computer sellers offer warranties lasting from one to three years that you can buy at the time of purchase. Find out whether an engineer will call on you if you have a problem.
- training for whoever is to use the computer – if the computer is to be used for management purposes (for example, for the accounts) you as proprietor of the business ought to have at

least a nodding acquaintance with the program used. The cost of training – also of getting your computer up and running – may be an obligatory part of the 'package' cost if you are buying an entire system for a specialised purpose.

Few businesses will find themselves spending less than £1,500 on a computer system. The cost will, of course, depend on your requirements, but £2,500 may be considered a likely figure for many businesses. If this sounds a lot of money to spend, bear in mind that the price of computer equipment has been falling year by year, yet its quality and power are constantly improving. Moreover, a computer properly used may enable you to run your business with fewer staff then would otherwise be required.

Choosing the hardware

The term hardware means the machinery used in a computer system. It includes the computer itself and extras, such as printers, modems (which enable computers to exchange information over telephone lines) and scanners (which copy images on to the screen).

Although the computer is only the first building block of a computer system, it will be by far the most important item bought, particularly since it will determine what programs are available to you. The most common of today's computers are 'PCs', descendants of the IBM PC originally introduced in 1981. Other computer systems, such as the Apple or Acorn ranges, have been developed independently with their own set of programs. PCs are the jacks-of-all-trades, with a massive range of software and compatible hardware available, while the others have a smaller range of software, much of it dedicated to specific areas, such as graphic design work or games playing.

In the PC world brand names are less important than technical specifications, which tell you how fast the computer works, how much working memory it has – too little can slow a computer to a crawl – and how much filing space it offers for software and your own information.

Speed is determined by the 'processor chip', which is the engine of the system. Chips are described by a variety of colourful technical-sounding names. Currently the choice is between Pentium

MMX chips, Pentium II chips, the Cyrix 6x86MMX (also known as the M2) and the AMD K6. Chips are also given a speed rating in MegaHertz (MHz). As a rough guide, the higher this number, the faster the computer will work, although absolute speed depends on a number of other factors.

Pentium II chips are too powerful and too expensive for typical business use. Any of the others are suitable for a business PC, although it is worth noting that computers based on the Cyrix or AMD chips will sometimes be slightly cheaper. A speed rating of 200MHz will be more than adequate for most tasks, although it may be wise to edge this up towards 250MHz or even 300MHz as the technology improves towards the end of 1998.

Filing space is provided by a 'hard disk', and is measured in gigabytes (Gb): 1.5Gb is a comfortable minimum. Working memory is shown in megabytes (Mb): 32Mb is a reasonable figure. Both filing space and working memory can be expanded easily and cheaply.

Various types of screen are available. Modern PC-compatibles use the SVGA (Super Video Graphics Adaptor) system, which can display both pictures and text with ease. Images appear as a grid of tiny coloured dots. The number of dots is known as the screen's 'resolution'. A standard SVGA screen uses a grid of 640 by 480 dots, each of which can be one of 256 colours. This is ample for everyday business use. You should consider a higher resolution (800 x 600 and upwards) and more colours (either 64,000 or 16.7 million) if you plan to use your computer for artwork or colour photographs.

Screens are also rated according to diagonal picture size, much like televisions. A 14" screen is ample for letter writing and accounts, but you may find you need a 15" screen or larger if you intend to prepare your own leaflets and promotional literature.

The cheapest type of printer is the ink jet, which sprays bubbles of ink on to the paper. The output can be either colour or black and white, and prices start from around £150. Laser printers are slightly more expensive (prices start at around £250) but produce much clearer and sharper output, and are also cheaper to run. The affordable models offer black and white printing only. Colour laser printers produce printshop-quality results, but still cost many thousands of pounds.

Once you have a computer, the door is open for you to use it in many ways you would not have originally intended, so it is a good idea to buy a system with enough memory and processing power to accommodate new programs in the future.

Choosing the software

The computer and its peripherals are the visible parts of the system. But without software – programs to tell them what to do – they can do nothing. There are two levels of software. On a low level is the operating software, which manages the computer's own resources. There are two options: MS-DOS, developed by Microsoft (now largely obsolete) and Graphical User Interfaces (GUIs).

GUIs were developed as an alternative to the text-based DOS by Apple (with its Macintosh computer), with the emphasis on making the computer easy to use. With GUIs, also known as mouse-and-pointer systems, the screen shows all of the software applications available as little pictures (known as icons), which you select by moving a hand-held unit called a mouse, which in turn changes the position of a pointer on the screen. If you want to open up another program, you do not have to close down the one you are currently in, but can simply open up the second one in front of it. This 'multi-tasking' is more like non-computer work, where you don't have to put away one thing just to glance at another for a moment.

The most common GUI found on PCs is Windows 95. An older version, called Windows 3.1, is now largely obsolete. Some business software still uses the much cruder text-only MS-DOS system; however, this can be used successfully with both versions of Windows. On Apple computers the current GUI is known as System 8. This is due to evolve into a completely different system, so if you are buying an Apple system make sure that the latest version of the operating software will work with the application software you plan to use to help you with your work.

In practice, it is this latter software that affects your productivity the most. You will need to investigate software that does some or all of the following:

- word processing, for writing letters and creating documents
- accounting
- sophisticated information storage and processing systems known as 'databases'
- stock control

- financial planning
- communications, to send information to other computers.

There are also a number of 'integrated packages' which combine word processing, database, spreadsheet and communications functions, but these often need a lot of computer power to run.

Your priority is to find the right software for your business needs. Almost every type of business has had software written for it at some time or other, but you will be best off using a tried and tested system if a suitable one is available. Make a point of asking how many other businesses use the same system, and try to arrange to see an existing system in operation before committing yourself.

Backing up data

Once a computer is turned off, all the information in the working memory is lost. Therefore, if you want to keep your work, you will need to save it.

Your computer will have a built-in hard disk which stores information when you are not working on it. There will also be a floppy disk slot, which can be used to add new software to the computer and to keep back-up (safety) copies of work and of the software you use. You should make sure that back-ups are performed regularly – at least once a day for important work – and that you keep safety copies of the software you use in a safe place away from the computer. Don't allow games or other non-business software to be used, as these programs may contain viruses – programs designed vindictively to destroy the information on your computer. You can buy virus killer programs (about £100) to combat viruses and check the health of your system.

If you need to back up a lot of information you should consider getting special hardware to help you. Options include:

- removable drives such as Zip and Jaz drives – these work like a hard disk but write information on to small cartridges. Prices start at £150 for around 100Mb
- tape drives, which write information to a special tape cassette. Capacities range from 750Mb to 4Gb. From around £150.
- CD writers, which store 650Mb of information on special blank CDs. CD writers start from around £300.

Networking

It is possible to connect computers in a small office together so that they can share information and extras such as printers and scanners. Putting together a networked system is not a job for a beginner. However, many mail-order companies and traders will be able to quote for a complete system which will come with all the extra hardware and software you need.

The Internet

The Internet offers a number of services which may be of interest to small businesses. The most useful of these are email, and the World Wide Web.

Email is very much like the letter post, but cheaper, quicker and more versatile. Messages are sent from computer to computer over the Internet almost instantaneously. Text can be copied to and from a word processor or other document, and it is possible to 'attach' images, sounds, and other kinds of information. For many applications email compares very favourably in both cost and speed to faxing, especially when sending information abroad.

The World Wide Web is both a research resource and an international notice board. Small companies can advertise on the World Wide Web very cost-effectively, while researchers and journalists can use it to get news and background information.

You should consider getting an Internet connection if you provide information that can be transmitted electronically (for example journalism or certain kinds of graphic design), if you feel you have a product or service that can be sold internationally, or if you need access to the latest news or research. The benefits for other kinds of businesses are less obvious, although it is likely that by the early years of the next century the Internet will be as widely used as the telephone and fax machine are today.

Practically, to use the Internet you need a telephone line, a computer extra called a modem which costs around £150, and a subscription to an Internet service, which will cost between £10 and £15 a month. Details are available from any of the Internet magazines which are now widely available.

Data protection

The Data Protection Act was passed in 1984 following widespread concern about people's private affairs being recorded on computers, with the attendant risks of inaccuracy and uncontrolled disclosure.

It is a very wide-ranging piece of legislation. It applies to information about living, identifiable individuals: not just sensitive information, but names, addresses and telephone numbers, even though these are to be found in directories. These data come under the Act if they are held in equipment which can process them automatically – for instance, a computer or word processor. (Note that under a new Data Protection Bill to be introduced, some non-computerised records will also be covered).

If you have a computer, you may need to register under the Act. A number of uses are exempt, for example a home computer used not for business but for family affairs, household accounts and so forth. In business, there are several exempt uses (calculating pay, keeping accounts or basic text preparation) but the exemptions are hedged with strict conditions. If any of these conditions are breached, the exemption is lost.

You must find out whether you will need to register. An explanatory booklet with application forms is available direct from the Office of the Data Protection Registrar.*

You may need to register even if you do not have a computer of your own: your accountant, or your computer bureau, may hold and process data for you, but you control the contents and use of the data. If you have spare capacity on your computer which you make available to someone else, you will need to register as a computer bureau.

Failure to register is a criminal offence for which the Registrar can prosecute.

When registered, you must always operate within your register entry (such as purpose, type of data, source, to whom they are disclosed). This is important as it is also an offence under the Act to knowingly or recklessly hold or use data in a manner not described by your register entry. In addition, you must comply with the eight Data Protection Principles. If you change your business address, you must inform the Registrar.

The register is open to public inspection. Any individual about whom data is stored (that is, held on a computer), is entitled to a copy of the information concerning him or her. A charge of up to £10 (for each register entry searched) may be levied for giving access to the information, and there is a 40-day deadline for providing the information. Proper precautions must be taken to make sure that the individual requesting the information is who he or she claims to be. If an individual suffers damage (that is, financial loss, or physical injury – hurt feelings by themselves are not enough) as a result of his or her data being inaccurate, lost, destroyed or improperly disclosed, he or she is entitled to claim compensation.

Many trade associations and chambers of commerce may be able to advise you; so, of course, can your professional advisers. Ask your accountant to add data protection to the checklist for your business, to make sure that you operate as registered, and/or to notify the Registrar of any changes.

The current fee for registration is £75. Registration lasts for three years, after which time a renewal reminder will be sent automatically.

Chapter 11

Protecting ideas and innovation

All businesses own potentially valuable 'intellectual property' and ought therefore to know the simple procedures necessary to safeguard and use this property. Unfortunately, patents and other intellectual property rights are all too often ignored by small businesses because they are perceived as being complex and expensive. In fact, a business can avoid time-consuming problems and can save money simply by learning the basic rules of intellectual property.

Intellectual property primarily protects ideas and innovations against copying and imitation but, used properly, can do much more. For example, a company wishing to develop a new product should begin by having a patent search made. The patent specifications found will prevent the company from wasting time and effort 'reinventing the wheel' by repeating previous work. It is also possible for the search to reveal an ideal new product which is freely available for adoption.

Some intellectual property rights are true monopolies and provide protection against competition even when no copying has taken place. This means that a company initiating a new project quite independently could find itself being sued for infringement of the rights of others. If such conflict does arise, it may be necessary to withdraw from the market and to pay damages.

The risk of coming into conflict with existing rights can largely be avoided by having 'freedom to use' searches made before any new product, service or logo is launched. If you find that someone else does have rights to something you were hoping to make part of your business, all is not necessarily lost; by applying for a licence for use of the invention, both parties could end up winning.

Intellectual property is the collective term used to refer to the laws designed to protect new ideas and innovations, namely:

- confidence
- copyright
- unregistered design right
- registered designs
- trade and service marks
- patents.

Confidence

All companies have information which they need to keep confidential. The recipe for Coca-Cola, for example, is a well-guarded secret. But more mundane company information, such as customer listings and next season's price list, needs to be kept from competitors. Confidentiality is also important because premature disclosure of the information to anyone who is not under a legal obligation of confidentiality can be a bar to the grant of a patent or registration of a design.

To use confidentiality, it is necessary to identify the information which is to be kept secret. Access to the secret should be controlled, and those who are to know should be under a duty to maintain the confidence. Employees generally already have such a duty, but should be reminded of it. Outside contractors should be required to sign an appropriate undertaking to keep the information confidential.

Commonly, competitors seek access to databases such as customer lists and mailing lists. It is helpful to be alerted quickly to any misuse of such material, and therefore address lists, for example, may contain 'fake' entries to provide early warning of the use to which a list is being put.

Copyright and unregistered design right

You will have seen copyright notices, for example, at the end of television programmes, or when loading a computer program, but may still fail to appreciate that copyright impinges on all aspects of business. Copyright exists in the original 'literary, dramatic, musical or artistic work'. Literary works include computer programs, letters, booklets, advertisements, instruction manuals, price lists, business plans and databases. More physical objects such as buildings and sculptures, photographs and drawings also all have copyright.

Copyright is automatic. Any work which is original in the sense that someone has expended skill and effort in its production has copyright, and once the work has been completed the copyright is there. The company only needs to ensure that it owns the copyright and that it can enforce it if necessary. This is simply a question of following the basic rules, which are:

- retain all original works. You could deposit a copy with your bank or solicitor or, to prove that the work existed by a particular date, send a copy to yourself by registered post, keeping it unopened
- ensure that all retained works identify the author and the date made
- ensure that the company owns the rights.

It is from the author of any piece of work that ownership of the copyright arises. If the author is an employee, and makes the work as part of his or her own duties, the company will own the copyright. Frequently though, advertising material, artwork, computer programs and other specialist works are contracted from outside. In such circumstances, agree at the outset who is to own any copyright which might arise, and record that agreement in writing.

Copyright is a right to prevent copying. If a competitor takes a short cut, for example, by issuing a leaflet which is the same or similar to one of your own, action can be taken to have the competitor's leaflet withdrawn and all copies destroyed. Furthermore, damages by way of compensation will be available. However, try to discourage copying by putting a copyright notice on original works made available to the public. Such a notice is the word 'copyright' or the symbol ©, followed by the year of publication and the copyright owner's name.

The length of time for which copyright lasts has recently changed. Copyright in a literary, dramatic, musical or artistic work (including photographs) now lasts until 70 years after the death of the author. Sound recordings, broadcasts and cable programmes are protected for 50 years, and published editions for 25 years. However, this applies only to works originating in the UK or most other European countries. In other cases, the term of protection is that given by the country of origin, which may be shorter.

Traditionally, manufactured products were also protected by copyright. However, since 1 August 1989, all such goods have been protected by the Unregistered Design Right (UDR). This provides limited protection for all manufactured goods, for example for furniture, engineering products, tools, containers, clothing, toys and models, office equipment, packaging, jewellery, stationery, and consumer goods in general. UDR is similar to copyright in that it arises automatically and is a right to prevent copying or imitation. However, in most cases UDR will only last for ten years from first marketing, whereas copyright can exist for much longer. As with copyright, a company has to ensure that it can enforce UDR if necessary. With UDR it is the original drawings or the first prototype of the new product which needs to be retained.

To avoid allegations of infringing copyright or UDR, make it a rule not to copy, and insist that products or services obtained from others are original. If a work is independently produced there can be no question of copyright infringement.

Registered designs

Although UDR provides some protection for industrial products, it is uncertain and is very limited in term. Therefore, reliance should not be put on this automatic protection for any projects of importance.

Where manufactured goods have a novel appearance, they can be protected by way of a registered design. This is a true monopoly, which can last for up to 25 years. To obtain a registered design it is necessary to go through an application process so that the Designs Registry at the Patent Office,* acting on behalf of the public, can satisfy itself that the application meets the necessary criteria.

To be granted a registered design it is a first requirement that the design is new, that is, that the product looks different from previous designs and has not already been sold or otherwise disclosed in the UK. This means that, in general, the application has to be filed before the product goes on to the market. However, in some cases it is still possible to obtain a valid design registration even after there has been some disclosure of the design, provided that less than 50 articles have been produced, and there have been no commercial dealings in the articles.

The second requirement is that the article should have been specifically designed to have an aesthetic appearance, or otherwise appeal to the eye. This is to exclude solely functional articles from registration. So, for example, office equipment and furniture which is sold on appearance is registrable, whereas functional items such as fuses and terminals are not.

Articles such as works of sculpture, wall plaques and medals, and printed matter such as calendars, greetings cards, maps, playing cards, etc., are specifically excluded from registration.

The application process to obtain a registered design is straightforward. It involves making a request for registration accompanied by drawings or photographs showing the article. It is considered by an Examiner of the Designs Registry and if there are no objections a Certificate of Registration is issued. Otherwise, the Examiner has to be persuaded by argument or amendment that any objections raised have been overcome.

When granted, a registered design enables the owner of the registration to stop anyone in the UK making, selling, using or importing articles with the same or similar design. The registration owner does not have to prove that the design has been copied, and it is immaterial that the infringement has been made independently.

Trade marks

A trade mark is a word or symbol which distinguishes the goods and services of one trader from those of others. It describes not the nature of the goods, but their origin. Thus, if a book carries the trade mark Michelin™, this does not mean that the book is made of rubber, nor is it about rubber products. The mark tells you that the French tyre company has originated or is in some way connected with the book.

Once a mark or brand has been chosen for goods and services, it is important, first of all, to ensure that the mark is free for use, that is, that using it will not infringe any existing rights. Thus, before a new mark is launched appropriate trade mark searches need to be carried out.

It is possible to acquire rights to a mark simply by using it, and where that use is so substantial that a considerable reputation has been built up, competitors can be stopped from using a similar mark by an action of 'passing off'. However, a strong brand is extremely valuable and ought to be protected even before goodwill and reputation have been accrued. This can be done by registering the mark. You have to register the mark in respect of specific goods or services – you cannot register a blanket right to it.

In order to register a trade mark it is necessary to make an application to the Trade Marks Registry at the Patent Office.★ A Trade Mark Examiner considers the application and, in particular, conducts searches to ensure that the proposed mark does not conflict with any existing registrations or applications in the pipeline. This means that an application for registration, and subsequently a registration, may also help to prevent competitors registering similar marks and serves as a warning to others of your rights in the mark.

Patents

Patents are the most powerful of all intellectual property rights. Like a registered design, a patent is a monopoly, but a patent protects much more than the visual appearance of an article. A patent can protect the basic concept of a project.

Patents protect 'inventions', that is, something that can be made or used in any kind of industry. This means that products, machines, methods of making products, testing products, and processes can all be protected by patents. However, a number of things are specifically excluded from patent protection, including discoveries, literary works, rules for playing games, methods of doing business and computer programs.

To obtain a patent the invention must be both new and non-obvious. An invention is new if, when a patent application is filed, it has not been made available in any way, to anyone, anywhere in the world. It is therefore vital to keep details of all projects confidential until it has been decided whether or not to apply for a patent.

An invention is 'obvious' if a person skilled in the field would think the invention trivial or an obvious development of what is already known. However, it is important not to confuse obviousness with simplicity. Patents are not necessarily about major breakthroughs, and many are granted every year for small improvements, for example to fixings, packaging and other everyday products.

To be granted a patent it is necessary to go through an application procedure so that the Patent Office★ can establish that the necessary criteria for a patent have been met. This involves filing at the Patent Office a request for a patent together with a patent specification. This specification has to include a technical description which is in sufficient detail to enable someone to make or perform the invention. This means that published patent specifications are an extremely valuable source of technical information. The patent specification also has to include at least one 'claim' – a statement setting out the scope of protection sought.

The patent application process is a step-by-step procedure, with the applicant having to initiate the various stages. During the procedure, an Examiner in the Patents Office makes a search through earlier patent documents to test the novelty of the proposal. Thereafter, the application is published to alert the public to its existence and to its contents. The final stage is essentially a negotiation process during which objections raised by the Patent Office have to be overcome by argument or amendment. Not all patent applications are successful.

Patents are often ignored by businesses in the UK on the grounds that patents are complex and expensive, and that 'my competitor will easily be able to get round the patent by making minor changes'. In fact, patents are extremely powerful business tools and the cost of acquiring a patent in the UK to obtain an absolute monopoly for 20 years can be less than the insertion cost for one quarter page advertisement in a national newspaper.

Intellectual property outside the UK

Intellectual property is international and most countries provide rights which are very similar to those of the UK which are outlined above. Thus, copyright is recognised in most countries and action can generally be taken against plagiarists around the world using copyright which has been originated in the UK.

For registered designs and registered trade marks it is generally necessary to make a separate application in each country where protection is required. Fortunately, this does not need to be done at the same time that the UK application is filed. Thus, under the terms of an international agreement, foreign design or trade mark applications can be filed and can be given the date of the first British application if such foreign applications are made within six months of the first British application.

Generally, when seeking foreign rights it is necessary to apply in each country individually. However, several systems now make it easier to obtain foreign patents. First, there is the European Patent Convention by which a single European patent can be obtained to cover up to 20 or so European countries, including the UK. Although the system is expensive it is a boon to those companies needing extensive protection in Europe. The International or PCT system enables a single application to be filed for nearly 100 countries worldwide.

A European trade mark system has been in operation since 1 April 1996. If you register your trade mark with the Office for Harmonisation in the Internal Market (Trade Marks and Designs),★ you can stop anyone using the same or similar trade mark on the same or similar goods anywhere in the European Union. However, it is more than likely that most small businesses will have no need for Community-wide protection – if you are just selling to one or two member countries it may be cheaper and simpler to register separately in the UK and in each of the other countries.

Getting help

The UK Patent Office publishes free information as to how to obtain patents, designs and trade marks, and this is available on request from the Patent Office.★ However, it is generally advisable to seek professional help and guidance.

The professionals who are qualified to advise in all intellectual property rights are patent agents or patent attorneys. Their professional body is the Chartered Institute of Patent Agents,★ which can provide free introductory booklets on patents, trade and service marks, and industrial designs.

You can find a patent agent from the *Yellow Pages* or from a regional directory available free from the Chartered Institute. But do make sure that you are dealing with a Chartered Patent Agent (CPA). Anyone, including the unqualified, is able to offer services in these areas.

A patent agent can apply for any of the intellectual property rights for you, can make searches to see if ideas are new, and to check your freedom to use new ideas and innovations, and can advise and act if things go wrong. Patent agents can also advise on agreements, licensing and other commercial dealings with such rights. Many firms of patent agents are also prepared to offer free preliminary advice, for example under the Chartered Institute's scheme 'Patent Agents for Innovation'.

The Patent Office's Search and Advisory Service★ can carry out searches for you. A full search to see if something can be patented costs around £500 to £800, while a simple search limited to computerised databases costs a minimum of £270.

If you wish to make patent searches yourself, the British Library Science Reference and Information Service★ has a comprehensive collection of British and foreign patents. Patent collections are also held in patent libraries in regional centres. Your local Business Link★ or alternative may be able to tell you what is available in your area.

Chapter 12
Being a retailer

Every high street is the same, every high street is different: para-doxically, both statements are true. From town to town, the first impression is of sameness, with the familiar chain stores and mul-tiples, Boots, W H Smith, Sainsbury's and many others in various combinations in every shopping centre of any size. But if you look more closely, you will notice among the famous fascias many belonging to the smaller businesses, with just the one shop, or perhaps one or two branches. And in villages and suburban shop-ping parades the individual businesses will be in the majority; some old-established, others recently started, all determined to keep their end up.

These are not easy times for retail businesses: the shopkeepers are fighting the huge organisations for a share of the customers' spending power, and are using considerable ingenuity in doing so. The multiples, with their enormous resources, vast floor space and the ability to command the whole output of a factory, have an undoubted advantage in cutting prices and offering a large variety of lines. The smaller shops that do not evolve and adapt to meet this challenge are fighting tanks with bows and arrows.

Some practise guerrilla warfare, turning their small size to advantage in offering the kinds of service that are not worth the big organisations' while: opening very early or staying open very late; delivering to customers' houses; and others. The small shop's strongest weapon is the element of service which is the one thing the giants cannot match. Many people prefer to spend their money where vegetables and groceries will be delivered, a dress altered to fit exactly, or d-i-y tools sold with some expert advice.

The small shop can sell goods in small quantities: one slice of ham, half a yard of elastic, six screws; in the big stores, such items are prepacked, giving the customer little control over quantity. Such a service is especially valuable to people whose needs are modest.

Having what it takes

Most people have idyllic childhood memories of playing shop: reality is quite a bit different.

It helps to be an early riser (especially in the food trade), such as a greengrocer who has to go to the wholesalers in the early hours, and be back in time to open the shop. Or there may be early morning deliveries to attend to, as in the case of a newsagent. You may not get to bed very early either, because accounts, stock control, VAT, ordering and credit card matters may all have to be dealt with in the evening.

The advice that you should acquire some working experience before setting up on your own applies doubly to shopkeeping, not only in order to learn some of the mechanics of the trade but to find out if you are temperamentally suited to it.

If your customers become irate, you will hear about it pretty soon. But no matter how you feel, you will have to appear unfailingly cheerful, patient, polite and helpful even when customers offer a good deal of provocation. An offended customer is unlikely to return.

Opening hours

Shop opening hours are unrestricted from Monday to Saturday. Following the Sunday Trading Act 1994, the only restrictions on Sunday opening now apply to large shops – those with an internal sales area of more than 280 square metres. Large shops can open on Sunday for a maximum of six hours provided they give notice to the local authority. However, they must close on Easter Sunday and, if it falls on a Sunday, Christmas Day.

There are some exemptions from the restrictions. Motor and cycle supply shops, off-licences, pharmacists, farm shops, and shops at airports, railway stations, petrol stations and service areas face no restrictions, whatever their size. There is a special exemption for shops occupied by Jews which close on Saturday.

Premises for a retail business

There is one common factor shared by almost all retail businesses: the need for a street frontage. Generally this means that the shopkeeper must find ready-built premises in a shopping centre (though if it is a new development, he or she may be the first occupier).

A trader needs to choose the right shop in the right location in the right district, and adapt it to his or her own needs.

Choosing the district

It is doubtful whether anybody chooses an area in which to trade completely at random. You, too, will probably have reasons of your own for wishing to open a shop in one part of town rather than another.

By all means use your inclination as a starting point, but keep an open mind: if your investigations show that the preferred district is a no-hoper, look elsewhere.

Find out, preferably by personal investigation over a period of time, whether the area is prosperous or declining. Try to find out what the unemployment rate is: closed-down factories are an ominous sign. Note 'For Sale' boards on private houses – if there are many, and they remain for a long time, there may be more people moving away from the area – or trying to – than are coming in. If there are many high-street shops for sale or rent, you will not have any trouble finding one, but you may not do much trade there.

Look at what other shopping centres there are nearby. It may be that the more prosperous residents, the ones with cars, are accustomed to take their business farther away, perhaps to some big, new shopping complex, so that you would have to make do with the shoppers who cannot manage or afford the journey.

Do people come to work in the district? Look for offices, schools, colleges, industrial estates: people who have to shop in their lunch hour seldom go far afield. On the other hand, if you mostly sell to people who commute in, you may be twiddling your thumbs on Saturdays, which elsewhere are the best shopping days.

Where there are any other reasons why people should come into the district – a swimming-pool, a central library, council offices, a museum or art gallery – all these can bring in potential customers from other districts. If there is a railway station or bus terminus nearby, the users may have to pass by.

Choosing the location

For a shop, nothing is more important than location. For most, the more prominent the location, the better, because although much of the custom may come from regulars, a good deal comes from passers-by, who are lured in on impulse.

A small shop in a small suburban shopping parade probably enjoys little passing trade and may have a captive clientele of local residents, particularly the mothers of young families, and the elderly. By staying open later than the high-street shops, it may attract people who work and those who have simply run out of something. If this is the sort of shop you want, finding premises will be largely a question of locating a vacant property. But be careful about competition: there may not be enough trade for two butchers or two hardware merchants.

In a high-street shopping centre, the presence of a competing business may not necessarily be a disadvantage; it can even be a good thing, up to a point.

Where there are several shops of the same kind in a shopping district, it encourages people to travel there; customers like the prospect of choice, an alternative source nearby, and that source could be your shop. For some kinds of shop, competition is a positive factor: book-shops and shoe shops, for instance. Book-buyers like to drift from shop to shop, browsing: a shoe customer will prefer to know that if the shoes he or she wants are not available in one shop, there is another shoe shop nearby. Estate agents, too, gain a collective benefit from being closely associated with each other – people tend to visit a number of agencies, so there is no harm in making it easy for them.

A specialist shop, such as a builder's merchant, or a musical instrument shop, whose custom hardly depends on passing trade, may do well enough in a side street: it will attract specialist customers by becoming known in the trade. You may be able to expand a specialist business in such a location by selling mail order as well as over the counter.

Every shopping street has its 'dead end', where the trade is slower and the shops are less prosperous and change hands more often. It is important to identify and shun this unlucky location (probably marked by a rash of 'For Sale' and 'To Let' boards).

Even in the 'live' part of the street, some locations can be better than others. If you are taking over a going concern, you have, obviously, less choice. But if you are buying or, more probably renting, vacant property to convert to your own use, give preference to one sited where people have to pause: next to a pedestrian crossing, a bus stop, or near a parking place.

Buying a going concern

If you decide to take over a shop which is at present trading, the first thing you will want to find out is the owner's reasons for selling. They may be genuinely personal – such as ill health, or retirement. Or they may be strategic: perhaps the owner has heard rumours of a huge new supermarket to be built nearby, or of a large local factory closing down, and is getting out while the going is good. Find out by questions to the planning authorities, and enquiries in the neighbourhood, what new developments are planned in the area. A new main road bisecting a shopping district can halve its trade. Designating roads as one-way can be almost equally bad for trade, if it discourages some traffic from entering the area. A new hyper-market or shopping precinct could be fatal.

Or perhaps the present owner simply has not been able to make a success of the business, in which case the question is – can you? You should not only scrutinise the shop's accounts, but, if possible, also observe the proprietor at work. The reason for his poor financial performance may be idleness, incompetence, understocking or overstocking, understaffing or overstaffing, poor choice of goods or of opening hours. Perhaps it is the location that is at fault, and no shop in that line of business could succeed there.

There are other considerations: if the fixtures and fittings are not to your liking, how much will it cost to refit the shop? There may be no choice whether to buy or rent the premises. When renting, which is more common, you must know how long the lease has to run, whether it is renewable and on what terms. In a repairing lease, the consequent dilapidation liability must be allowed for in financial planning.

There is also the problem of what the goodwill is worth. A shop which is doing poorly cannot claim much of that, but even if it is doing well you cannot be sure that the customers are regulars who will transfer their custom to you.

You must, of course, have the property valued by a professional valuer and its leases and accounts thoroughly inspected, before coming to a decision.

These considerations are discussed in more detail in Chapter 5.

Starting a new business

You may be looking for an empty property in order to start a completely new shop. Where such a property is brand-new, in a newly built development, it may be difficult to assess your potential custom. But you should at least inspect the district; ideally, the development should include new housing or be near a residential area or a commuter area.

If you are thinking of taking over empty premises previously used as a shop, find out why the previous owner closed down: perhaps this is one of those 'dead' sites where no business ever succeeds.

You will have to clear any change of use with the local authority's planning department. But if you intend to carry on a business of similar character to the previous one, there is likely to be no problem. Most retail businesses are considered as interchangeable, and you can freely convert from one kind to another without permission. However, if you carry out any structural alterations to the building, your plans must be approved in the usual way.

You should consult your fire safety officer and some kinds of businesses, such as garages, which have special fire hazards, have their own regulations.

Accepting Luncheon Vouchers

If you sell pre-prepared food in any form, from full restaurant meals to snacks and sandwiches, and you want to accept Luncheon Vouchers, you have to make sure that they are used for food only, though the term 'food' includes any component of a bona fide meal, such as a canned drink (but not alcohol). Luncheon Vouchers Limited* will send you full details and display signs for your windows.

You have to count the vouchers and take them or send them to the company for reimbursement. There is a service charge on the redemption of the vouchers; this varies from 1.4 per cent to 1.9 per cent, depending on the volume. There are also service charges, depending on the speed of reimbursement for which you opt.

Buying stock

This is the heart of the matter for any shopkeeper who invests a large proportion of capital in stock, and, therefore, must buy it wisely.

How much to stock

Some products deteriorate rapidly (flowers, bread, green-groceries); others do not spoil with keeping, but go out of fashion (clothes, shoes). Even when they neither spoil nor date (most hardware), if nobody buys them, they bring in no profit with which to buy new stock, and take up the space needed for this stock. So, in every case, a rapid turnover of stock is desirable. Stock unsold is cash tied up or lost.

Do not be tempted to overstock, perhaps by an attractive quantity discount, nor to diversify too much.

It is essential to have some form of stock control system to track your sales and wastage and to guide your purchasing in future. The ideal is to buy only what your customers want, and to buy no more of it than you are able to sell. Depending on what you are selling, you may be able to offer an ordering service for products you do not normally stock. You need to weigh up the competitive edge this may give you against the extra administration and possibly poorer margins: there are often surcharges or reduced trade discounts for small orders.

You could buy through a symbol group, if you belong to one; or from a wholesaler; or from a cash-and-carry warehouse (a kind of retailers' supermarket); or directly from a manufacturer. They are not mutually exclusive. You might think that your orders are unlikely to be large enough to qualify for the quantity discounts which the manufacturer makes available to buying organisations and wholesalers, but do not dismiss the idea of buying direct from manufacturers.

Symbol groups

Some shopkeepers, particularly in the grocery trade, take on the big battalions with their own weapons by joining a voluntary symbol group which is a retailers' buying organisation (such as VG, SPAR,

Mace) in order to secure the large discounts that manufacturers offer to bulk-buyers.

Retailers agree to take a certain amount of goods each week from the designated wholesaler for their area and receive better terms than they would get on their own, and possibly other advantages such as a fascia with the group's symbol and the shop's name, help with the layout and fixtures, national promotions and advertising. In some cases, start-up help is given: the wholesaler may give the newcomer help in finding a shop and finance for it.

Details of the relevant head offices and wholesalers are listed in the *Grocer Marketing Directory*★ available from the publishers (or try your reference library). The trade press, mainly grocery, but also, for example, hardware, also carries such information. The applicant shopkeeper must offer some evidence of financial security, such as a bank reference. If he or she is already in business, the wholesaler will inspect the premises to see that they are in line with the organisation's requirements.

If there are other shops belonging to the particular symbol group in the neighbourhood, the wholesaler may refuse to take on another. Members of the group must undertake to purchase at least a specific amount regularly, and to stock a certain number of the organisation's own-brand products, but are free to buy goods from agencies other than the designated wholesaler.

Buying direct or from wholesalers?

When you first open your shop, if you are in a price-competitive field, it is important to try to open with a bang, not a whimper. Your opening offers should be good, and as the initial stocking of the shop is likely to be your largest single stockbuying for a long time, you may qualify for a quantity discount on this order. This is also the time to establish contact with the representatives of the major firms (probably four to eight) whose products are likely to account for a large part of your turnover. The manufacturers' representatives will have a good idea of what are competitive retail prices for the particular products, and may help you to reach them by means of promotional allowances or by providing redeemable 'money off' coupons for customers.

Obviously, you must check that you are not overlooking other sources of supplies that are cheaper, by joining a symbol group and finding a good cash-and-carry source.

Plan your opening carefully: there is no second chance to make a good first impression. Choose about 20 top selling lines and be prepared for very low profit margins on these. They can be from a mixture of sources; choose the best items from each.

When stocking your shop initially, you may be able to negotiate extended credit from your supplier, perhaps no payment for two months, then one-sixth of your opening order to be paid for over the following six months.

An advantage of dealing direct with the manufacturer is that if there are damages, the reps have facilities for exchange or credit which a symbol group or cash-and-carry store may not afford to you. A keen rep can use these facilities to give the retailer a little extra discount on purchases. You should be aware that damages eat into profit margins just as outdated stock does.

It is possible that manufacturers are less likely to run out of stock than a buying group – and lost sales lead to lost customers. But an advantage of indirect buying, if you stock many items, is cutting down on the time it takes to accept and check deliveries: much of your stock will arrive on one van, or, in the case of a cash-and-carry, be collected by you from one address. There will also be a considerable saving in paperwork.

What to stock?

There is, of course, no single answer to the question of which products and lines you ought to stock. It is partly commonsense, partly flair, and partly experience – so here, too, it helps to have worked in the trade.

Customers hardly ever give prior notice of their wants, but expect to find what they want when they want it. And if it is not there in your shop, they go somewhere else, rather than wait for it to be ordered. So the shopkeeper must keep on his or her toes, trying not to run out of anything, especially the most popular lines.

This demands keeping proper records and a constant check on what goes out, plus efficient and far-sighted reordering, which takes account of the fact that manufacturers do not always meet delivery dates, and that wholesalers have been known to run out of some products. A computer with the appropriate software can help in stock control (and at the same time indicate the profitability of various types of stock).

You must store your stock in such a way that it deteriorates as little as possible and does not acquire that grubby, shopworn look which is so off-putting to customers. You must rotate it, making sure that articles bought at the earliest period are put on sale first. Some food products are marked with 'sell by' dates, or shelf-life limits, and become unsaleable once these dates have passed.

Goods which have failed to sell or have passed the peak of saleability should be marked down in price, or thrown away, if perishable. Apart from taking up space fruitlessly, they create a bad impression. You might hold a seasonal sale or sell off unwanted stock week by week, or even day by day, depending on the goods.

Display

When you think of shops, you think of windows, their distinguishing feature. No other kind of business depends so much on visual display to attract customers.

What is essential is that the display should appear fresh, uncluttered and up to date: not dusty, crowded and superannuated. The window should be well lit, as eye-catching as possible, and changed fairly often. If there is any item that you want to promote specially, it should have pride of place.

Prices should be clearly marked, whenever possible. Leaving off price tickets does not encourage people to come inside to ask the price: it is more likely to make them suspicious and put them off.

If you decide to make your shop self-service, the goods must be easily accessible and each article marked with its price. And you must make sure that the check-out will not create a bottleneck.

When you acquire a shop, the previous owner's fixtures and fittings may suit your purpose exactly, but it is more probable that you will want to make some changes, if only by redecorating. If you are changing the nature of the shop's trade, you will want to start from scratch.

Plan this carefully beforehand, making a list of your requirements and a provisional sketch of the layout; then get estimates from several firms of specialist shopfitters, choosing the one that offers the best value for money. Visit any relevant trade exhibitions (see *Exhibition Bulletin*★, in reference libraries, for dates), that concentrate on shopfitting, self-service and display equipment. Use your buying group facilities and choose the best that you can afford.

Fittings have to last a long time and penny-pinching at the initial stage might prove expensive later.

Preventing theft

You cannot make your shop burglar-proof, but you can make it harder to burgle. Before you start trading, consult the crime prevention officer at your local police station and your insurance company. Insurers may lay down security precautions before agreeing to insure you, even to the extent of specifying that a minimum of two able-bodied people should take cash to the bank. You could perhaps get a good security firm to inspect the premises and install all necessary devices, such as locks and/or bolts on all doors and windows (not forgetting the basement and the attic) and a burglar alarm. But make sure that what you do does not conflict with the fire prevention regulations.

Other precautions include great attention to locking up; every key accounted for at all times; a light left on all night. Leave the till open at night – a thief would open it anyway, causing unnecessary damage, so most insurance companies insist on this. Do not have large sums of money in the shop at any time – get it banked. After banking hours, use the night safe.

If you do happen to be burgled, good stock control will pay off, as you will find it easier to list what has been stolen, which will help in getting your claim settled more promptly.

Pilferage by staff

This can be anything from a hand in the till to stealing from stock. By and large, it is the bigger firms' problem: supermarkets have the highest rate of shrinkage. The small shop run by the owner and his family needs less internal protection. But there should be rules about employees' own purchases from the shop.

Although it is difficult to know who is trustworthy, you should be as discriminating as possible about whom you employ. Demand, and take up, references. Having to practise eternal vigilance, constantly checking the deliveries, the stock, and the till is a nerve-racking business and not likely to improve relations with staff. Experience will help to teach you what precautions are necessary.

Shoplifting

This is more of a problem if the shop has a self-service layout, or if the goods are displayed on stands or racks (as in many clothes shops). You will hardly be able to afford to employ a shop detective, but it might be worthwhile to consider renting a closed-circuit TV system; you will get back some of the cost in tax relief. Often the presence itself of such a system is a deterrent. Place the monitor screen so that it can also be seen by customers.

Strategically placed mirrors, perhaps convex ones, can help at a modest cost. The shop itself should be well lit, with no murky corners, and shelves or racks of goods should have full light on them. Expensive pocketable items can be chained to the stands: perhaps electrically connected so that a buzzer sounds if the chain is removed.

Advice on these and other anti-theft devices can be sought from a security firm specialising in shop protection.

Vigilance is essential, but however suspiciously a customer may be behaving, do not challenge him or her until they have removed an article from the premises. Only if theft has taken place, and you have good grounds for suspecting who did it, can you make a citizen's arrest of a shoplifter. If you 'arrest' someone and then he or she is acquitted, so that no theft has been proved to have taken place, the arrest would be unlawful and you could be made to pay heavy damages.

Learning the law

The shopkeeper must comply with a number of laws, both civil (such as the Sale of Goods Acts, the Unfair Contract Terms Act and the Supply of Goods and Services Act 1982) and criminal (such as the Trade Descriptions Act 1968 and the Fair Trading Act 1973). The Consumer Protection Act 1987 deals with certain civil and criminal matters.

Other relevant criminal legislation includes the Food Safety Act 1990 and the Weights and Measures Act 1985: these form a series of special rules and regulations which apply to food.

All these pieces of legislation aim at enforcing the principles of fair trading. Advice can be sought from each local Trading Standards Department.

Sale of Goods Acts

The sale of goods legislation has guided the relationship between the seller and the buyer for over a century. The Sale of Goods Act 1893 was the first piece of legislation actually to set down in writing the legal position existing between the seller and the buyer in a contract for the sale of goods, and now, the Sale of Goods Act 1979, as amended by the Sale and Supply of Goods Act 1994, provides the foundation of the present law. The law currently gives protection to each buyer by implying certain rights or terms (known as conditions) into every contract for the sale of goods. The most important of these are that:

- the goods correspond with the description applied to them – whether orally, on the container, packaging, wrapping, labelling or other advertising
- the goods are of satisfactory quality – that is, that they are durable, safe and free from minor defects
- the goods are fit for the particular purpose – that is, not only must they work properly and be well made, but fit for the particular purpose that the buyer wants them for, whether that is an ordinary, everyday purpose or an extraordinary or unusual one. For example, a carpet may be of satisfactory quality but quite unsuitable for use in a specific location; but when the shopkeeper sells it to meet a specific requirement, it must be reasonably fit for the purpose specified. If the shopkeeper does not know whether or not the commodity will meet the customer's specific needs, he or she should make it clear that they do not know and therefore cannot advise the buyer.

Second-hand, reduced and shop-soiled goods are all protected by the requirements of the Sale of Goods Act. Such goods may be imperfect, but the buyer is entitled to fair value for the money he or she has paid for them.

The shopkeeper, too, is afforded some measure of protection and the buyer has no right to claim that goods are unsatisfactory where:

- the shopkeeper specifically drew the buyer's attention to the faults or defects being complained about before the sale was made, or
- the buyer examined the goods before the sale was made and should have seen the faults or defects being complained about for himself or herself.

Breach of any of these conditions amounts to a breach of contract, and it is for the shopkeeper to put the matter right. The customer is entitled to reject the goods, to reclaim the purchase price in full and to claim compensation for any loss or damage that has happened as a direct result of the contract being broken, such as the cost of re-papering and painting where a faulty cooker has exploded causing damage to the kitchen walls and ceiling. Afterwards, the shopkeeper can make a similar claim against the supplier or the manufacturer, being now the aggrieved party.

The precise time limits for returning goods which do not meet the requirements are undefined. Customers must merely exercise their rights within a 'reasonable' amount of time after purchase, with what is 'reasonable' depending on the facts of the case, and the type of goods. However, customers have the right to examine the goods properly before the right to reject them is lost: for example, if a set of skis is bought at the end of the season, and faults not discovered until the following winter, it is still possible to reject them. If goods are not returned promptly, the right to reject them is lost, but there may still be a right to compensation, such as the cost of a repair.

Where there is nothing wrong with a product as regards description, quality or fitness, and the buyer simply changes his or her mind about it, there is no legal obligation on the part of the shopkeeper to give a refund, or even an exchange. If the shopkeeper does so, it is purely a gesture of goodwill.

Unfair Contract Terms

The Unfair Contract Terms Act 1977 is concerned in part with restricting or preventing the trader from avoiding his or her liability towards a customer by using exclusion clauses in contracts. Attempts to exclude liability for goods which do not fit their description, are not fit for the purpose for which they were bought, and are not of satisfactory quality, are void under the Act. In contracts with traders, the effectiveness of such exclusion clauses depends on whether a court regards them as reasonable. In all contracts, any clause excluding liability for death or personal injury caused by negligence is void. Clauses excluding other liability for negligence can be assessed as reasonable or not.

Other clauses subject to a reasonableness test are those which try to get out of accepting liability for the loss of articles left for servicing, or for the late delivery of goods which were promised by a certain time.

The Act, however, allows an exclusion clause in dealings between the shopkeeper and the manufacturer, but only where that clause is a reasonable one. The Act itself sets out guidelines as to the test of reasonableness to be applied, and if a manufacturer wishes to rely on any particular exclusion clause, the burden of proof will be placed on him or her to show that the clause is fair and reasonable in the circumstances.

Exclusion clauses are not the only contract terms which require special care. Under the Unfair Terms in Consumer Contracts Regulations 1994, a consumer is not bound by an unfair standard term in a contract with a seller or supplier.

'Standard' terms are those which are set in advance, not negotiated individually with the customer, and typically they are found in the printed conditions of business on the backs of invoices or quotations. However, those terms which define the main subject matter of the contract and its price are not covered unless they are unduly difficult to understand, nor are terms which are explicitly required or permitted by law.

Broadly, an 'unfair' term is one which unduly weighs the contract against the consumer and in favour of the business. The business might have a defence, however, if it could show that it had acted in good faith, e.g. by ensuring that the consumer fully understood the term, and agreed to it freely without having been pressured to do so. The Regulations include a list of terms which could be regarded as unfair: these include a right to terminate without notice, a right to increase the price, penalty clauses and restrictions on legal remedies. A guidance note including this list (OFT 143) is available free from Office of Fair Trading Publications.*

Supply of Goods and Services Act 1982

The Supply of Goods and Services Act brings into statute law the various sorts of protection which the consumer has previously enjoyed under common law. Goods supplied as part of a service, on hire, or in part exchange, must fulfil the same conditions (such as being of satisfactory quality, fit for the purpose, conforming to description) as the Sale of Goods Act lays down for goods that are being sold.

The Act also sets out clearly that the customer should be able to expect any service paid for to be carried out with reasonable care and skill, within a reasonable time and at a reasonable price (unless a fixed time or a fixed price has already been agreed between the parties).

Where the service takes the form of a particular skill – such as, for example, a hairdresser providing a cut and blow-dry – the reasonable standard of care and skill required would be that expected of a reasonably competent member of the hairdressing profession. The work done in providing the service must have been authorised by the customer, and the retailer cannot expect payment for work done over and above what had been agreed between the customer and himself or herself.

In Scotland the same consumer rights exist but are covered by common law.

Further reading

Booklets giving an outline of the basic consumer rights can be obtained from the Office of Fair Trading Publications.* Although nominally addressed to shoppers, they contain much useful information for traders about their various obligations to customers.

*Croner's** Reference Book for Self-employed and Smaller Businesses* includes explanatory notes on selected Acts of Parliament. It should be available in most reasonably large reference libraries.

Law for Retailers, by Jennifer Brave, published by Sweet & Maxwell, sets out the key areas of law as they apply to retailers, and contains details of legislation of direct relevance to retailers, including sale of goods, trade descriptions, bargain offers, credit, consumer safety, theft and related offences, and negligence.

Receipts

The practice of giving the customer a written receipt as proof of purchase is a fundamental one to the retail business, but in common law there is no legal obligation on the part of the retailer to give a receipt, nor for the customer to produce one. The absence of a written receipt does not mean that the goods have not been paid for – the receipt could have been lost, or the shopkeeper may have omitted to give one in the first place. The law allows the shopper to prove his purchase not only by written proof (such as a till receipt or the customer portion of a credit card voucher) but also verbally (by 'parole evidence' – simply stating that he or she bought the items from that retailer). If payment is made by cheque, the law regards a cheque as a receipt, once it has been paid by the bank.

This is why the law forbids the shopkeeper to put up notices and display signs, or their equivalent, saying such things as: 'Refunds cannot be given in the absence of a written receipt,' which imply to the customer that complaints will be dealt with only on written proof of purchase. Statements like this are illegal, and the shopkeeper cannot rely on them.

Fair Trading Act 1973

The criminal law imposes further limits or restrictions on the shopkeeper relating to statements he or she may wish to make to customers, by virtue of the Consumer Transactions (Restrictions on Statements) Orders 1976 and 1978. These also apply to the manufacturer of goods, and have their origin in the Fair Trading Act 1973.

The Orders make it a criminal offence for a shopkeeper or a manufacturer to 'cut out' the statutory rights – as to satisfactory quality, fitness for the purpose, and conforming to description – afforded to the customer by the Sale of Goods Act 1979, whether by means of a display notice, a written contract, a wrapper, label, packaging, advertisement, or the goods themselves.

For this reason, each of the following statements is illegal and you can be prosecuted in respect of each of them: 'no money refunded', 'for hygiene purposes, goods cannot be returned or money refunded', 'sale goods, no money refunded', and 'credit notes only for faulty goods'.

Breach of the Orders is a criminal offence, which is punishable by fine, imprisonment or both. Enforcement of both is carried out by the Trading Standards or Consumer Protection Department.

Trade Descriptions Act 1968

The law of trade descriptions is of tremendous importance. Breach of it is a criminal offence, punishable by fine, imprisonment or both. Enforcement is the duty of the local Trading Standards or Consumer Protection Department, whose duly authorised officers have the power to make test purchases, enter premises and inspect and seize goods and documents for the purpose of determining whether or not the law is being complied with. Any person who wilfully obstructs a Trading Standards Officer, or who wilfully fails to comply with a valid request by such an Officer, or who without reasonable cause fails to give any other assistance asked for, commits the offence of obstruction.

Trading Standards Officers will also be pleased to provide guidance and advice, should you wish to consult them.

The 1968 Act creates a basic set of criminal offences by generally prohibiting false trade descriptions. It makes it an offence for anyone running a business to describe goods falsely and to sell, or offer for sale, goods so misdescribed. It applies to all aspects of retailing and includes advertisements, display cards, illustrations, labelling, packaging, brochures, ticketing and statements made verbally.

It covers descriptions as to quality, quantity, size, method or process of manufacture, composition, performance, fitness for purpose, testing, approval by any person, previous history of the goods, place or date of manufacture or processing, and by whom made.

Section 14 of this Act makes it a criminal offence for the trader to make a statement which he or she knows is false relating to the provision of services, accommodation and facilities. For instance, if a trader provides an invoice stating he or she had carried out certain repairs to goods and these have not been carried out, an offence may have been committed under this section.

If things go wrong, and proceedings have been taken against you for supplying or offering to supply services to which a false trade description is applied, you have a defence if you can prove that you did not know, and could not with reasonable diligence have found out, that the services did not match the description, or that the description had been applied to the services in question. This defence does not apply if you are supplying goods.

Whether it is goods or services you are supplying, you have a defence in cases where an offence has been committed through mistake or an accident, or through reliance on information supplied to you, or through the act or default of another person, or some other cause beyond your control. You must show that you 'took all reasonable precautions' *and* 'exercised all due diligence' to avoid an offence being committed. In other words, the shopkeeper must have a system in operation to avoid the commission of any offence, and that system must be effective.

Pricing

Under the Resale Prices Act 1976 it is unlawful for someone to supply you with goods only on condition that they will not be sold for less than a certain price, or to try to impose a minimum price by threatening to withhold supplies or discriminating in other ways. Suppliers can suggest a resale price provided that there is no indication that this is a compulsory minimum price, and provided you suffer no reprisals if you sell them for less.

The Office of Fair Trading regularly receives complaints of unlawful price fixing and is keen to help small traders to stand up to powerful suppliers who are ignoring the law. If you have evidence of price fixing, contact the Office of Fair Trading.★

Misleading price indications

The Consumer Protection Act 1987 created a general offence of giving a misleading price indication, which covers goods, services, accommodation or facilities. This is buttressed by various regulations which give more specific rules. Clearly, retailers are bound by the rules and to break them is a criminal offence, punishable by a fine.

In defining what it means by the word misleading, the 1987 Act covers the following five areas:

- indications about the actual price that the consumer will have to pay (for example, a retailer will commit an offence if he or

she indicates a price for goods which is lower than the price he or she is actually going to charge)
- indications about any conditions attached to a price
- any indications about the way in which a price will be calculated
- indications about what is expected to happen to a price in future
- any indications concerning price comparisons.

Several defences are provided by the 1987 Act. These include: compliance with any applicable regulations approved by the Secretary of State for the purposes of the 1987 Act, including the Price Indications (Method of Payment) Regulations 1991 (see page 192); the defence of 'due diligence', namely, that the retailer has taken all reasonable steps and exercised all due diligence to avoid committing the offence; and other defences, such as that for a publisher or publishing agent.

Enforcement of the law on prices is the responsibility of the local Trading Standards or Consumer Protection Departments and, as with the Trade Descriptions Act 1968, authority is given to make test purchases of goods, to enter business premises and to inspect any goods and to seize and detain goods where appropriate. Power is also conferred to examine any procedure connected with the making of the goods. As before, failure to allow a Trading Standards Officer to carry out his or her legal duties is a criminal offence – namely that of obstruction.

Code of Practice for Traders on Price Indications (DTI Nov 1988)

The purpose of this code is to 'put the meat on the bones' of the pricing law by setting out what is good trading practice to follow, so helping the trader to avoid the pitfalls of giving a misleading price indication.

Compliance with the code is important since it has 'evidential status', which means that if a trader is taken to court for giving a misleading price indication, the court can take into account whether or not the trader has followed the code. If he or she has followed it, that will not be an absolute defence, but it will 'tend to show' that the trader has not committed an offence. Failure to follow the code may make it difficult for a trader to establish the 'due diligence' defence given by the 1987 Act.

The code covers a number of areas, each of which is important. In any comparison with the trader's own previous price:

- the previous price should be the *last* price at which the product was available to consumers in the previous six months
- the product should have been available to consumers at that price for at least 28 consecutive days in the previous six months
- the previous price should have applied (as above) for that period at the *same* shop where the reduced price is now being offered.

Where these conditions are met, the price indication is unlikely to be misleading. Where the previous price in a comparison does not meet one or more of these conditions, the code requires the trader to give a clear and positive explanation of the period and the circumstances in which that higher price applied (this is not always necessary for perishables). The explanation must be displayed clearly, and as prominently as the price indication. The following is an example of the kind of explanation envisaged by the code:

January Sale
£4.50
Previous price £9
from 10 to 31 December

Other examples of the kinds of explanation required are also given, such as: 'These goods were on sale here at the higher price from 1 February to 26 February', or 'These goods were on sale at the higher price in 10 of our 95 stores only'. General disclaimers should not be used, and all comparisons shown should be fair and meaningful, and should always state the previous price as well as the lower price.

The code covers comparisons with recommended retail prices and other similar descriptions. A recommended retail price is defined as meaning a price which has been recommended to the trader by the manufacturer or supplier as a price at which the product might be sold to consumers, that price not being significantly higher than prices at which the product is generally sold at the time the trader first makes that comparison, and there being a normal commercial relationship between the trader and the manufacturer or supplier.

In addition, the code expressly advises against the use of initials or abbreviations to describe the higher price in a comparison unless the trader uses the initials 'RRP' to describe a recommended retail price, or uses the abbreviation 'man. rec. price' to describe a manufacturer's recommended price. The code states that all other price descriptions should be written out in full, and shown clearly and prominently with the price indication.

The code advises caution in describing offers as introductory offers, unless the trader intends to continue to offer the item for sale after the offer period is over, and to do so at a higher price. An introductory offer should only run for a reasonable period, otherwise it becomes misleading to describe it as introductory. By way of guidance, the code specifies that 'reasonable' relates to a matter of weeks, not months. Further guidelines are that an offer is unlikely to be misleading if the trader states the date that the offer will end, and keeps to it. A trader who extends the offer period must make it clear that this has been done.

If you want to quote a future price as part of the price comparison, the code advises that an 'after-sale' price or 'after promotion' price should only be used if you are certain that you will continue to offer identical items at that price for at least 28 days in the three months after the end of the offer period, or after the offer stocks run out. If you do quote a future price, do not use initials such as 'ASP' or 'APP' to describe it: the words should be written out in full, and be clearly and prominently displayed with the price indication.

The code advises you against comparing your prices with an amount of money described as 'worth' or 'value'. (For example, it would be in contravention of the code for a retailer to say: 'Worth £10, our price £5.')

Consult your local Trading Standards Department for advice on any of the requirements and, in turn, be prepared to cooperate with the Department and respond to its reasonable requests for information and assistance. Copies of the code may be obtained free from the DTI Consumer Affairs Division.★

Further regulations on price indications

The Price Marking Order 1991 requires the selling price of goods offered to consumers to be indicated in writing. The Order applies to virtually all goods sold in the course of the provision of a service, food sold and consumed in catering establishments, antiques and works of art.

The selling price can be shown on the goods themselves, on a ticket or notice near them or grouped together with other prices on a list in close proximity to the goods. The unit price must be shown for goods sold from bulk or pre-packed in quantity. The Order also lays down which goods must be priced in metric measures, and those for which imperial measures can still be used.

VAT must be included in the price if the customers are mainly private consumers, but VAT can be shown separately from the basic price if the trader is selling mostly to business customers. Additional charges which the customer has to pay, such as delivery, must be included in the price displayed or be shown with equal prominence.

There are special provisions relating to jewellery, precious metals, motor fuel and goods sold by mail order.

The Price Indications (Method of Payment) Regulations 1991 concern retailers who charge different amounts for goods or services depending on the method of payment (e.g. adding a percentage for payment by credit card or a fee for payment by cheque). The trader must state the methods of payment to which any indicated price does not apply and must specify the difference between the marked price and any other price as a percentage or as an amount of money. This information must be given by notices placed at public entrances to the premises and at points of payment. Items may also be marked individually with two or more prices.

You can be fined for failing to comply with either of the above regulations. Enquiries should be addressed to the DTI Consumer Affairs Division.*

Origin marking

Traders are required to state the origin of imported goods only if they are presented in a way which would give consumers the impression that they were made in a particular place and were not, in fact, made there. The legal duty, then, is to correct a misleading impression given as to place of production or manufacture. The use of a trade mark or use of a particular language will not, in itself, attract this legal requirement, but it may do so if the trade mark or use of language is likely to mislead.

Breach of this requirement is a criminal offence, punishable by a fine or up to two years' imprisonment, or both. The Department of Trade and Industry has produced a set of guidance notes for traders on the law – the Trade Descriptions (Place of Production) (Marking) Order 1988. Copies are obtainable, free of charge, from the DTI Consumer Affairs Division.*

The general safety requirement

The Consumer Protection Act 1987 introduced a 'general safety requirement' for consumer goods supplied in the UK. This makes it a criminal offence to supply consumer goods which are not reasonably safe. Penalties can result in a fine or up to six months' imprisonment, or both. The general safety requirement applies to anyone who deals in consumer goods which are not reasonably safe 'having regard to all the circumstances', and these circumstances include such aspects as the manner in which the goods are marketed; any warnings or instructions given with them; the means, if any, and the cost of making the goods safe; and any published safety standards.

An important defence exists especially for the retailer, that he or she neither knew, nor had reasonable grounds for believing, that the goods failed to comply with the general safety requirement. The Secretary of State also has the power to make safety regulations which set out in detail how specific products must be constructed, and what instructions and warnings must be given. Examples are regulations covering the flammability of upholstered furniture. For information on specific products contact the Department of Trade and Industry.*

Enforcement of the general safety requirement is the responsibility of the local Trading Standards Departments, which have been given increased powers for this purpose. Not only may they seize goods which offend against the new requirement, but they may also issue suspension notices, so prohibiting suppliers from selling offending goods, and they may further apply to the courts for such goods to be made forfeit and subsequently destroyed.

Product liability

The Consumer Protection Act 1987 introduced into the UK the provisions of the European Community Directive on Product

Liability. This brought into force the concept of strict liability (that is, liability without fault) for defective products (not just consumer goods). Under the 1987 Act, liability is channelled towards the producer, the importer and the (own-brander) of the product. In certain limited circumstances, other suppliers may be liable, and this could include the retailer.

For further reading on this subject, you should obtain a copy of the free DTI *Guide to the Consumer Protection Act 1987 – Product Liability and Safety Provisions*, obtainable from DTI Consumer Safety Publications.*

Giving customers credit for goods or services

As a business person, you are perfectly free to give credit to a customer for goods or services which you have supplied to him or her: that is, you can agree to allow him or her to defer payment. Or you may inform the customer that credit will not be available.

A creditor is not obliged to give a customer reasons for refusal, but if he or she has consulted a credit reference agency, the customer can demand to know the name and address of that agency – to enquire of it as to the information which it holds.

Consumer Credit Act 1974

The Consumer Credit Act 1974 and its subsequent Regulations set down the rules to be followed in dealing with credit – particularly in relation to licensing, credit references, credit cards or tokens, credit advertising, the giving of credit quotations and agreement forms for documenting credit transactions.

The Act regulates most of the agreements under which credit is advanced to any person (but not where credit is advanced to a limited company), regardless of whether the credit agreement is a hire purchase, a conditional sale or a credit agreement in respect of services rendered or goods supplied. It applies whether the person supplying the goods or services provides the credit facility or refers his or her customer to a finance house.

The Act imposes strict rules on the advertising of credit. It also gives customers the right to require a written quotation, clearly stating the exact terms on which credit is on offer, although this right is rarely exercised.

Consumer credit business

Any business which provides credit under credit agreements which are regulated by the 1974 Act is called a consumer credit business, for example a shop selling goods on its own credit terms or a finance house which supplies or finances goods under hire-purchase agreements.

Credit agreements

Before providing credit or hire facilities (such as renting out television sets or cars) you will need to ask your customer to sign an agreement, setting out his or her rights and obligations. In many circumstances, the customer has the right to cancel the agreement: if so, the agreement itself must contain a notice explaining the customer's legal rights. Certain provisions are in force which require various copies of the agreement to be given to the customer. You should always be aware of them.

The Consumer Credit Act lays down detailed rules for the information to be given in an agreement form, and the statements of the customer's rights which must be shown.

Licences

Licensing is an essential part of the legal requirements on credit, and a person who carries on a consumer credit business must first obtain the appropriate credit licence. (If not, he or she commits a criminal offence.) The period during which a consumer credit licence has effect is now five years, but it can be varied, suspended or revoked by the Office of Fair Trading where the concept of 'fitness' is put in doubt. There are currently six categories of credit licence, namely for:

- category A – consumer credit business
- category B – consumer hire business
- category C – credit brokerage
- category D – debt adjusting and debt counselling
- category E – debt collecting
- category F – credit reference agency.

A credit licence is not granted automatically, and each application is vetted by the Office of Fair Trading. The Director General of Fair Trading must be satisfied that the prospective licence holder 'is a fit person to engage in activities covered by the licence' and that 'the name(s) under which he applies to be licensed is (or are) not misleading or otherwise undesirable'. Details of all licence applications are kept in a public register. If an application is turned down (which seldom happens), the shopkeeper can appeal. An appeal, on a point of law, can also be made to the courts.

Apply for all credit licences, and the leaflet *Do You Need a Credit Licence?*, to the Office of Fair Trading, Consumer Credit Licensing Branch.★ Licence application forms are also generally available from local authority Trading Standards Departments.

A shopkeeper will need to have a Category A licence – which covers those situations where credit is offered to the customer. A shopkeeper without a licence who endeavours to enter into any credit agreement will not be able to enforce it against the debtor unless he or she obtains an order from the OFT permitting him or her to do so. It will, in certain circumstances, be necessary for the shopkeeper to obtain a Category C licence where he or she enters into 'credit brokerage'.

Credit brokerage businesses

Any business which introduces individuals who want credit to other businesses offering such facilities is a credit brokerage business. So, if you do not sell a TV set on credit terms but refer your customer to a company which provides credit facilities, and handle the necessary paperwork, you are operating a credit brokerage business, and as such you must obtain a Category C licence.

Canvassing

It is a criminal offence to canvass credit agreements for cash loans in people's homes unless the trader has a written invitation to visit, made before such facilities were discussed. Any trader who wishes to canvass credit agreements for the supply of goods and services off trade premises needs a special category of licence to permit this.

Further reading

Because consumer credit legislation is very intricate and involves so many regulations and calculations, you should obtain and read very carefully the information booklets, brochures and leaflets obtainable free of charge from the Office of Fair Trading.★ They include:

Credit Charges (how to calculate the total charge for credit and the annual percentage rate of charge); *Regulated and Exempt Agreements*; *Advertisements and Quotations Regulations*; *Cancellable Agreements* and *Non-cancellable Agreements*; *Hire Agreements*; and *Matters Arising During the Lifetime of an Agreement*.

The Consumer Credit Trade Association★ publishes a series of short guides providing guidance on the Consumer Credit Act. It also provides training to its members to meet requirements connected with all aspects of credit, and publishes detailed information on new legislation. It provides a personal advisory service to members and sells standard documents complying with the Consumer Credit Act. Its members receive a bi-monthly journal, *Consumer Credit*. The annual membership fee for a new company is £211.50 including VAT.

Chapter 13

Getting paid

Late payment eats into profits and can be a big problem for small businesses, particularly if it is a major customer who fails to pay up on time. One survey suggested that the average payment period was 50 days, although the most common payment terms are for payment in 30 days.

Attempts are being made to improve the situation. Publicly quoted companies now have an obligation to give details of their payment performance in their annual report and accounts, and the Federation of Small Businesses★ is proposing to develop league tables, in collaboration with Dun & Bradstreet,★ the business information company.

The Labour Government has gone further, to propose legislation which would give businesses a statutory right to interest on late payment. However, opinion is divided as to whether this right will really help in practice – you may be reluctant to claim interest if it will jeopardise your relationship with a major customer. Government departments and local authorities are also being required to pay on time.

As always, prevention is better than cure, and possible cash flow problems should be taken into account when deciding what forms of payment to accept, whether your customers are mainly retail and the sums involved small or whether the sums involved are large. The DTI booklet, *Make the Cash Flow* (URN 94/553), available free from DTI Small Firms Publications,★ is a useful introduction to the various ways of dealing with the problem.

Retail customers

Cash

Virtually all retail businesses still rely in large measure on cash transactions. While there is no certain way to avoid forged notes, there are steps you can take to reduce the risks.

Ultra-violet lamps to detect forged notes are available, but not foolproof – forgeries are supposed to fluoresce under them, but perfectly legal notes may also do so if they have been in contact with certain detergents.

A more reliable guide is to compare a suspect note with another which you know is genuine – for example, a genuine note should feel crisp, not limp, waxy or shiny, the watermark should be hardly apparent until the note is held to the light, and all genuine Scottish and Bank of England notes have a thread embedded in them which should appear as a bold continuous line when held up to the light. The Bank of England* produces various leaflets which further explain security features.

Cheques

When you accept a cheque, there is always a possibility that it may bounce, unless you insist that the customer produces a cheque card, and write its number down on the back of the cheque. This guarantees payment if you took the cheque in good faith and you can insist on the bank paying up, to a set limit (either £50 or £100) even if the chequebook and card should turn out to have been stolen, or if the customer's account is empty. You cannot get round the limit by taking two or three cheques for single purchases costing over the limit: this invalidates the bank's guarantee of the cheque card, and possibly none of the part-payment cheques would be honoured.

Do not accept any other identification, such as a driving licence, since it does not guarantee the owner's solvency. Do not accept cheques for more than the limit stated on the card without checking with the customer's bank, or holding up delivery of the goods until the cheque has been cleared.

Accepting plastic cards

If your goods carry a profit margin reasonably in excess of the credit card companies' commission (at present around 4 to 5 per cent for smaller businesses), you may decide to try to attract more customers by becoming a merchant of one or all of the principal credit card organisations: American Express, Diners Club, Master Card or Visa. There is also the option of accepting Visa Delta or Switch cards as a plastic alternative to cheques. From the retailer's point of view, these work in a very similar way to credit cards, but with a different charging structure: there is a handling fee for each transaction, which could be as much as £1 or £2.

When you have signed an agreement with a card company, you will be supplied with instructions on the acceptance of cards and either an imprinter and vouchers or an electronic terminal.

Certain checks are necessary every time a card is presented: making sure the card is valid (the expiry date has not passed); that the card has not been notified to you as lost or stolen; that the amount is within the 'floor limit' advised to you by the card company (if it is in excess, you will need to obtain authorisation); and that the signature of the customer on the sales voucher agrees with the signature on the card. Details of the card are then recorded on the voucher by use of the imprinter or by swiping the card through an electronic terminal.

You may be given an envelope in which to send your vouchers to the card company; or you may hand them over to a cashier at a bank as you would cash or cheques.

One of the advantages of an electronic terminal is that you do not need to deliver vouchers to the bank, nor phone up to ask for authorisation for large sales (the terminal does this automatically). However, you have to pay to buy or lease a terminal, and you should check who is responsible for insuring it.

You will receive a monthly statement from the card company, summarising all the transactions submitted, and indicating the service charge due, which will be deducted from your account by direct debit.

Plastic card trading is not appropriate for some forms of retail trade, such as small food shops or others where the margin of profit is low, because of the card company's service charge or commission.

Plastic card fraud

The holders of credit cards, such as Barclaycard, Master Card, American Express, Diners Club, or debit cards such as Visa Delta or Switch, are supposed to notify the issuing organisation as soon as they discover a card to have been lost or stolen. If you accepted a stolen card in good faith, however, the issuing organisation will pay you the money. The card company may send you details of stolen cards from time to time, with instructions not to accept those cards. The number of cards which you are asked to check at any one time is kept to a minimum – but it may still be difficult for a shop to check every single card that is offered.

Electronic terminals should check cards automatically – but you cannot rely on them completely because of the delay before the computer's records are updated.

Card companies pay rewards for lost or stolen cards which are picked up by shops, but may refuse to accept transactions resulting from the use of cards which have been listed as stolen.

Card payments by phone or post

From the point of view of the fraudster, shopping by mail or telephone with someone else's card details is ideal. It is less so for the trader. If you inadvertently make a sale to a fraudster and the genuine cardholder disputes the transaction, the card issuer is entitled to 'charge back' the transaction to your account, even if you obtained authorisation, for no other reason than because the cardholder disputes the transaction.

You should take extra security measures to reduce the risks. Because there is no card to imprint in such cases, you have to enter the details (customer's card number and its expiry date, the name and address and amount charged) on the card slip. For mail order sales, the customer's signature should be on the order form: for telephone sales, make a note of the time of the conversation.

In order to reduce the risks (you cannot eliminate them), send the goods only to the cardholder's address: do not let a third party such as a 'courier' collect them. If the cardholder collects the goods, you should ask to see the card and get the signature. For large-value transactions, you could offer to ring back customers after checking details with directory enquiries. To confirm that the goods have been received, you could insist on some proof of receipt.

Avoiding problems

Forged notes, bouncing cheques and stolen cards all eat into your profits. For information about shoplifting and other forms of theft see Chapter 12. With all forms of theft, it is a good idea to monitor your losses so that you can take action if you see any trends emerging; joint action with other shopkeepers nearby may bear dividends. For example, you could set up some sort of 'early warning' system whereby you all agree to alert each other if someone you suspect of passing forged notes is sighted. Different police authorities work in different ways, but it may be worth contacting the local Crime Prevention or Crime Reduction Officer to see what advice they can give. In any case, you should certainly ensure that your employees are trained to follow the correct procedures – without putting themselves at risk – if they do encounter a suspect customer.

Larger amounts

While payment with an order may be the ideal, it is often not possible – either because it is not normal practice in your line of business, or because you are supplying trade customers. If so, you can still reduce the risks of late or non-payment. For example, although full payment up-front may not be acceptable, a deposit may be, particularly for a new customer.

Discounts for early settlement are possible, but expensive: you need to weigh up the speed of payment against the loss of profit. And, if customers make deductions they are not entitled to when they pay their bills, it can be difficult to recover the money. An alternative is to make future discounts conditional on prompt payment. Whatever incentives you choose, you should always state your terms of business when accepting an order. Ensure that your invoices are equally clear in stating the goods or services for which you are charging, the order reference number, payment period, payment method, and expected payment date, and set up a regular system for chasing outstanding debts. A professional approach to credit management will not harm your reputation.

There are various ways of assessing your customers' creditworthiness before you let them have high-value goods or services. Getting to know your customer's ability to pay can be combined with your marketing research. Keep a record of the individual who actually makes the decisions, and their position, as well as any other contacts and any visits you have made to them. Do not underestimate the value of the grapevine – other businesses in the area may know of impending problems with a particular customer.

You can ask for a bank reference. The bank will charge for this, and will need permission from their customer. Ask specific questions such as 'Do you consider XYZ good for £5,000 on 30-day terms?' and be aware that the reference will speak in what is effectively a coded language: for this reason, you should not place sole reliance on them.

Credit agencies are in the business of providing details of potential customers, their financial results, the payment experience of other suppliers, county court judgments, outstanding loans and a credit rating. You can either take out a subscription to a database, or buy reports on a one-off basis. Reports start at about £12 for the simplest, and rise to about £35. However, there may be an extra charge for a one-off report: you may be able to avoid this by getting a report through your local Business Link,★ many of which have their own subscriptions.

All these precautions offer no guarantee that payment will be made. It is possible to buy credit insurance to guard against bad debts. The British Insurance and Investment Brokers Association (BIIBA)★ can give details of specialist brokers.

Factoring

If you are in real cash flow trouble, perhaps because you have reached your bank borrowing limit and have a lot of customers owing you money, you could think about factoring. The factoring company advances you the money owing on your customers' invoices (usually up to 80 per cent), and retains a percentage as commission when they are paid.

Consult your accountant or Business Link★ for the name of a suitable company. Most factoring companies are backed by clearing banks or other major financial organisations. One disadvantage is that there is usually an administration charge or service fee which depends on volume. Firms with lots of low-value invoices may find that this fee makes factoring uneconomic.

Factoring traditionally used to be a last desperate attempt to raise money, but is now becoming a much more acceptable and commercially viable way of raising finance.

It is still an expensive way of buying money but can be helpful in relieving some of the administrative burden involved in chasing invoices and ensuring that slow-paying customers do not lock up your working capital.

As a rule of trading, you should do all you can to induce those who owe you money to pay as quickly as possible, while paying your own bills on time. In both cases, much is at stake: a loss of trust can sour relationships with your customers, or mean that an important supplier refuses to supply you.

You can obtain *A Guide to Factoring and Discounting* (URN 95/685) from DTI Small Firms Publications.★

Chapter 14

Exploring some dreams

There are some businesses that have an enduring appeal for people hoping to become their own boss: having a bookshop; keeping a pub; being a newsagent. These seem to require no special training, and they bring you into contact with things which are generally associated with pleasure: alcoholic drink, magazines, tobacco, sweets, books. An employment agency has the appeal of dealing with people, something for which many people believe themselves to have a natural flair.

Being a bookseller

Many people have a fantasy of keeping a bookshop because they like books. What is more, they may imagine that they will start off by selling, second-hand, all those surplus books now on their own shelves at home. The reality is not so.

An enthusiasm for books is not enough. Running a bookshop has its perils and pitfalls as well as its rewards. An understanding of retailing in general is essential, as well as a good knowledge of the way the book trade works, in order to make a success of running an independent bookshop at a time when the chain and multiple bookshops are growing in number and in strength.

Publishers offer the retailer set discount rates, which are normally 35 per cent but vary from publisher to publisher, and from book to book. Net profit in bookselling is notoriously low. Larger orders carry larger discounts, but it is a gamble to buy-in a large number of copies on the chance of a potential bestseller. No bookseller can stock more than a fraction of the hundreds of thousands of titles in print.

Until recently, booksellers were shielded from the full force of price competition by the Net Book Agreement, which ensured that most books were sold at the same price in all outlets. The Net Book Agreement collapsed in 1995 and was ruled unlawful in 1997, so booksellers can now fix their own prices. Since the larger chains are in a better position to discount prices, it is vital for small independent booksellers to use the full range of marketing skills.

Choosing a stock that sells is a key skill: an independent bookseller needs to learn what to stock for the needs of the community he or she serves. Many independent bookshops are successful because they provide a good service, or devote themselves to specialising in a particular area (such as children's books, medical texts, history, cinema, etc.). Others widen their market by offering a mail order service in their specialist area.

The Booksellers Association of Great Britain and Ireland★ offers advice, information and training. Joining allows you to participate in the Book Tokens Scheme (open to members only) and the Booksellers Clearing House, a central clearing facility which enables booksellers to pay a large number of publishers' monthly accounts in one single payment.

The Association also has available a free leaflet, *Starting a Bookshop*, aimed at new entrants to the trade who need to know about the workings of a bookshop. The Association negotiates preferential rates for members on many essential services such as insurance, credit cards and parcel delivery.

Keeping a pub

Not all publicans are self-employed – many are managers working for the brewery. To be self-employed, you must either own a free house or, more commonly, rent a public house from a brewery. For this, in the first place write to the brewery of your choice, ask for an interview and give details of yourself and your husband/wife, your experience in the licensed trade (if any) and the amount of capital that you have readily available for investment in the pub. The available capital might have to be any amount between £10,000 and

£100,000 to buy the stock and necessary equipment and give some working capital.

Breweries are selective about tenants, and prefer married couples who will work as a team. You are unlikely to be considered if you are over 55 years old. It is an advantage to have worked in the trade and have had some specific training, apart from general knowledge of retail business. It is not enough to have been a devoted customer. The Brewers & Licensed Retailers Association* publishes a free leaflet called *Thinking of Running a Pub?*.

A pub has to be licensed by the local justices and if you become its tenant you have to apply to be named as the licensee. The application goes to the magistrates who hold licensing sessions at regular intervals but a protection order can be granted to give temporary authority to carry on the business until a new licence is granted.

If your application to be a tenant is accepted by the brewery, you will be required to enter into a tenancy agreement which, among other things, requires you to buy all your beers from the brewery (although tenants of a national brewery can buy cask-conditioned beer from a source of their choice). The agreement may also require you to buy your wines, spirits, cider and minerals from the brewer. All the profits on the sale of food and liquor remain in your hands.

The work of a publican is hard and requires a capacity for appearing good humoured at all times, while keeping a sharp eye on both customers and staff; short-changing or overcharging customers, or giving friends double measures or cheap drinks is bad for business.

Being a newsagent, sweetseller, tobacconist

Running a small shop that sells mainly newspapers is not an easy life, nor outstandingly lucrative. Before you take over an existing shop, apart from the usual checks about the lease and the standing of the business, you must ensure that the wholesaler who is supplying the existing owner will continue to supply newspapers and magazines to you when you take over the shop. There is nothing automatic about this.

There may be a limitation on the number of papers that you are allowed to buy on sale or return, and some magazines are supplied on firm sale only. So you might find yourself with unsold stock.

You will need to stay open on every day on which newspapers appear, which is about 360 days of the year. Some newsagents, normally those who do not operate a delivery service, close on Sundays, but this makes for lost sales.

You must be up before the lark every day, taking delivery of papers, sorting them and marking them up if you operate delivery rounds. Among your headaches will be sending out bills to tardy customers, and explaining to customers why their newspaper or magazine has not arrived – which may be due to industrial action at the publishers or wholesalers.

If you do home deliveries, you must find schoolchildren to do your rounds and will have to deal with the local education authority inspectors. There are by-laws about employing children to deliver newspapers; children must be at least 13 years old, you must get a permit from the local education authority and adhere to rules such as those about the earliest and latest times that rounds can take place. There are also special health and safety regulations, which are covered in Chapter 8.

Sweets and tobacco, being tempting, pocketable and anonymous, are readily stolen. Selling requires sharp-eyed vigilance both in the stock room and in the shop.

You will have to deal with numerous suppliers offering many lines, so there will be the need for constant stock checks and reordering. This is where access to a computer might help, especially as the prices you are allowed to charge tend to change with surprising frequency.

It is not unusual for a newsagent to work a 90-hour week and do no better than just make a living.

An employment agency

It is important to realise that an employment agency is not easy money, and needs people who are willing to face quite tedious work, and have not only drive but also a vast amount of patience and good sales skills. It is necessary to have, or acquire, proper training in interviewing, backed by a good knowledge of the industry or area in which you intend to operate.

Before starting an agency, consider what type of agency you intend to open – office agency or secretarial and clerical staff and probably temporary staff in the same categories; or a specialist agency, for example computer staff, nursing staff, accountants, or engineers. For specialists, it is important for at least one of the directors or partners to have a good knowledge and understanding of the types of jobs which occur in the particular area of work.

When planning to set up an agency, be sure to carry out adequate market research beforehand, because you will be operating in a highly competitive market. And do not make the mistake of thinking that you can run an employment agency in your spare time, after your ordinary day's work is finished.

Getting the clients

Building up contacts can be achieved by telephone or personal calls, or via literature about your business. Calls are likely to be better because the initiative is then yours, not the client's.

A small agency must build up personal contacts and operate on a personal basis but this cannot be rushed, and immediate first-name familiarity on the part of the agency is not always the way in.

It is important always to tell your client the truth about prospective candidates and not to hard-sell the applicant, so that the client will have confidence in your opinions on candidates, and will trust you – which is vital. It is no good sending unsuitable applicants to clients in the hope of doing business.

Recruiting the applicants

If your premises have a shop front, display the job vacancies for temporary and permanent staff in your windows. Alternatively, and in addition, it is a good idea to advertise permanent job vacancies in a local paper or, for specialist agencies, a national paper or specialist journals. The wording of the advert should aim to bring in not a quantity, but the right quality, of applicants: the type of candidates who can do the job that is advertised. If you keep a record and analyse your responses from different media, you may learn which are the best to use for a particular type of vacancy.

Money matters

If you have temporary workers, you will need a fair amount of capital because you pay the temporary staff straightaway at the end of each week (at an agreed fee per hour, tax and insurance deducted) and although the hourly charge to the client is more (by how much depends on the category of staff), payment from the client may not come in for several weeks.

For permanent staff, you charge an introduction fee of 10 to 15 per cent of the annual salary. But when you first start an agency, the people whom you place in permanent jobs sometimes do not start their employment immediately, which can result in something like six to eight weeks, or more, passing before you are paid any fees.

Formalities

You do not need a licence to run an employment agency (unless it is a nursing agency). Even so, the Employment Agencies Act 1973 lays down a number of standards of conduct which must be met.

Running an employment agency involves a great deal of record-keeping to comply with these standards. There is probably enough record-keeping, paperwork and bookkeeping to keep one person fully occupied.

It is also important to have a good broad knowledge of the various statutes and regulations concerning employers and employees.

The Federation of Recruitment and Employment Services Ltd★ can give some preliminary advice on running a private recruitment consultancy, and will forward an information pack about the FRES on request. It is the trade association for the private recruitment service, and gives advice on terms of business, documentation, insurance and legal matters to its members.

The Institute of Employment Consultants★ offers courses in employment consultancy and all aspects of agency work and sets examinations for recruitment specialists, including the Certificate in Recruitment Practice (operated jointly with the Associated Examining Board), as well as a correspondence course leading to a Foundation Vocational Award in employment agency practice. The IEC acts as an advisory body for recruitment specialists from a wide variety of fields.

Chapter 15

Becoming an exporter

A manufacturer who has a product that is competitive in the UK market, but who is looking for another way of increasing business, may achieve the growth needed by selling goods abroad. At the same time the manufacturer will be spreading his or her risks, since even if there should be a world recession, it is unlikely that all countries will be equally affected, and being able to manufacture in larger batches may also make him or her more competitive in the home market.

It is also possible to export without manufacturing, by becoming an export merchant or export agent, and selling abroad goods bought from manufacturers in the UK.

You must pick your markets intelligently, and do some basic research to find out which countries are most likely to want to import what you have to sell, rather than trying to export bacon-flavoured crisps to the Middle East; or goods made from prohibited materials in another country according to their national regulations; or goods which do not comply with that country's standard specifications.

Selling abroad carries the same problems as the home trade, plus some others, such as: arranging the packing and shipment of goods to countries perhaps half-way round the world; complying with a great variety of foreign import regulations; securing payment in a world of shifting currency values and methods of payment. The exporter must be ready to cope with the unforeseen at home (such as a dock strike) and abroad (such as a revolution).

Exporting is not something you can fit into the odd moments you can spare from other concerns. If you plan to manufacture for sale both at home and abroad, either directly or through agents, you will need staff trained to deal with all aspects of exporting, and must be prepared to spend possibly several months a year travelling overseas yourself.

If your resources do not run to this, you might do better to sell overseas through an export intermediary – commonly called an export house – while you concentrate on building up the manufacturing side of your business and developing your domestic market. The British Exporters Association (BExA)* can assist you in contacting appropriate intermediaries through the *Directory of Export Buyers in the UK* (see below) and the periodic *Export Enquiry Circular* in which, for a nominal charge, you can place a notice detailing your product. This will then be seen by all the Association's export house members, and those interested will contact you direct. The British Exporters Association estimates the cost of setting up your own competent export department at some £60,000. But it need cost you nothing to use an export house.

When your export business is on a firm footing, you can gradually build up your own export unit: for instance, by employing part-time, retired export specialists, and by training existing staff. The Institute of Export* provides an Export Specialists service, and education and training in exporting.

Export houses act in a number of capacities. They may run an import/export business themselves and pay you in the UK on shipment. They may act as an agent of the UK exporter or, as a 'confirming house', they may represent an overseas manufacturer. Confirming houses place orders with UK manufacturers on behalf of their overseas principals or buyers. A confirming house will pay a supplier on shipment, and will, if necessary, extend credit for up to 180 days to the overseas importer. You must register your willingness to act as a supplier with appropriate export houses: the *Directory of Export Buyers in the UK*, published by Newman Books*, lists over 800 export houses. The 1997 edition costs £85 plus £5 postage and packing, but a reasonably large reference library should have a copy.

If you plan to become an export merchant or agent yourself, you will be wise to start with only one or two kinds of goods. Make yourself thoroughly familiar with them, and do not extend your range until you are well established in the trade. Capitalise on any reliable contacts overseas, such as family members.

Exporting, step by step

Most of the basic steps are the same whether you are dealing with goods manufactured by yourself or by some other firm.

Deciding where to export

Your first inkling of a possible market may already have come to you, in the shape of unsolicited enquiries from abroad; or friends in the trade may have mentioned some possible opening. From these, and sources such as the trade press and newspapers, you can pick out one or two possible markets, then you need to do some desk research to find out the most hopeful.

The DTI offers a wide range of help, advice and support at each stage of the export process. Much of the information comes from the Foreign Office (more properly, 'Foreign and Commonwealth Office' or FCO for short), which feeds through to the DTI commercial information from embassies and consulates abroad. Your first point of contact for advice on what is available should be your nearest Business Link★ (some of which have export counsellors), Government Office (in England), Scottish Trade International, the Welsh Office Exports Branch, or the Industrial Development Board for Northern Ireland. In addition, there are 'country desks' at the DTI,★ which provide information on particular countries, such as import duties, local taxes and exchange controls. Country desks work closely with 'Export Promoters' – experienced exporters seconded to the DTI from the private sector.

The Export Market Information Centre (EMIC)★ is provided by the DTI to help British exporters in carrying out desk research. It holds a variety of information on overseas markets. Sources available include overseas statistical publications, foreign trade and telephone directories, some market surveys of overseas markets, and mail order catalogues and development plans. The staff can carry out research on your behalf, for a fee.

The DTI also publishes a range of export publications giving background information on a specific market or a more detailed look at the opportunities for particular products or services within that market. Telephone DTI export publications★ for a catalogue of export publications. If you are planning to sell in Europe, there is also a DTI Euro Hotline★ providing information on export issues within Europe, and a network of European Information Centres (ask at your nearest Business Link or Government Office).

Other sources of information are Chambers of Commerce, foreign diplomatic posts in London, the trade press, and the business sections of the national press. You should also contact an organisation called Technical Help to Exporters★ (part of the British Standards Institution), for advice on technical requirements for products in foreign countries: the first half hour of help is free, after which there is a charge. A leaflet giving all the details is available on request.

Developing the market

When you have found one or two markets that look promising, make sure that your product or service fits the need of those markets. Among the services available is help towards the cost of overseas market research through the Export Marketing Research Scheme operated by the British Chambers of Commerce (BCC)★ on behalf of the DTI.

The DTI notifies UK businesses of overseas opportunities. Sales leads are identified from a variety of sources including Foreign and Commonwealth Office commercial staff overseas. These opportunities are made available to subscribers of a matching service run by Prelink Ltd or to those who access the data remotely on a database operated by FT Profile. Details can be obtained from the DTI country desks★ (see 'Deciding where to export', above).

By correspondence and by visits to the markets, you should try to find channels of distribution; these can vary from direct sales to individual outlets, to having your own marketing company. There will probably be companies with established operations who are prepared to help you, for agreed terms. To explore overseas markets, you could join a trade fair or mission, some of which are supported financially by DTI grants: the BCC produces a trade mission handbook. Alternatively, simply get in touch with the commercial attaché, at the embassy in the country of interest.

It is worth finding a good agent in each market (the DTI can help you with this): you must then give the agent full back-up support. The DTI may also be able to provide a report on the local standing, probity and representational capacity of overseas companies. You will need to develop suitable promotional material. If it is to be in a foreign language, it should be prepared by a native speaker who also has some relevant technical knowledge. The Languages in Export Advisory Scheme (LEXAS), run by the BCC on behalf of the DTI provides grants to help exporters pay for specialist consultants to analyse all their overseas trade communications.

It is important to have a watertight agreement with each overseas agent. The International Chamber of Commerce★ has a model agency contract; contact it for details.

Securing a profit

To ensure a profit from overseas sales, it is important to have reliable channels of distribution. So take professional advice: from a freight forwarder, about the terms on which you should trade; from a broker, about insuring shipments; from the international division of your bank, about handling payment. SITPRO★ (the Simpler Trade Procedures Board) also has a helpdesk for procedural, payment and documentation queries.

You may also need to secure yourself against export credit risks by taking out insurance (see 'Protection against export risks', at the end of this chapter), but if you can, avoid taking such risks when you first start to export. Many overseas buyers expect credit, therefore risks cannot be entirely avoided.

Managing the operation

It is unlikely that anyone will place an order without first receiving a quotation. To save time, send this promptly in the form of a pro-forma invoice.

A pro-forma invoice looks like an ordinary invoice, except for the words 'pro-forma' in the heading. The figures you quote are binding. The invoice should indicate the type and quantity of goods, with details of their prices, the delivery time, the terms of payment (such as letter of credit or sight draft), the currency in which the deal is to be made, and the method of packing. It should also state which 'Incoterms' (standard trade terms) apply, for example:

f.a.s.	– free alongside ship
	price includes delivery to the docks (named port)
f.o.b	– free on board at named port
	price includes delivery on board ship

CPT	– carriage (paid to . . .)
	price includes freight charges, but not insurance charges, to a named port of destination
CIP	– carriage and insurance (paid to . . .)
	price includes both freight and insurance charges to an agreed port of destination.

All the terms should be clearly set out in the quotation or pro-forma invoice, because once the customer has signified his or her acceptance of this, it becomes a contract binding on both parties. Hence, you should also state how long your offer remains valid. If an order has been confirmed by the customer by fax, email or telex, you should also get confirmation by letter; pro-forma invoices must also be sent by post.

Dealing with suppliers

Unless you are the manufacturer of the goods, or have them in stock, when you receive an enquiry, you will need to contact the manufacturer or stockist for quotations. You must emphasise that the goods will have to be suitably packaged for export. The supplier's quotation or pro-forma invoices should be with prices quoted f.o.b. or CIP, as requested.

If a supplier will only quote f.o.b., you must ask for an approximate shipping specification: the number of packages, cartons, cases, etc. that will be needed, the delivery time, their gross and net weights and their shipping measurements. You need this information to estimate the cost of freight, and insurance if required, plus the shipping expenses which the forwarding agents will charge. Your supplier's terms of payment may be cash with order or cash within seven days from receipt of invoice (possibly with a special cash discount); or monthly account (subject to satisfactory trade and bank references); or some other method of payment.

Be meticulous in comparing your supplier's quotation with the pro-forma invoice you send to your potential customer overseas. Any discrepancies between the supplier's descriptions and the customer's requirements must be sorted out because, once the order is placed, the customer will usually insist on receiving the goods exactly as specified in the pro-forma invoice. Any confusion about whether the prices quoted are f.o.b., CIP or so on can play havoc with the calculations of an exporter's profit.

Croner's★ *Reference Book for Exporters* contains a wealth of information about all aspects of the export trade, with separate entries for every country, giving a summary of its individual import regulations. Use it to check that your freight forwarder is giving you good advice. It should be available in a reasonably large reference library.

Arrangements for shipment

For sending goods by sea or air you will normally need the services of a freight forwarder, who should be a registered trading member of BIFA, the British International Freight Association.★ The freight forwarder will advise you on the best method of transportation to your destination, depending on your requirements as to speed, safety and cost, and will quote for the cost of freight and other charges, prepare most of the shipping and customs documents, arrange marine insurance, if required, and attend to other shipping details.

When the goods have gone forward to the ship, the forwarder will obtain bills of lading – detailed receipts for the goods, issued by the shipping company, and containing a contract whereby the company undertakes to deliver the goods to a specified port of destination.

The bill of lading is the most important part of the transaction, being a document of title to the goods listed on it, but is now increasingly superseded by the non-negotiable sea waybill, which is not a document of title; it enables the consignee to clear the goods without acquiring a title to them.

In the deep-sea liner trade, goods are now generally moved in containers, which may contain several different consignments, and be packed inland, before being moved to the docks. Goods to short-sea destinations, such as the Continent, are usually moved on road vehicles straight on to the ferries ('ro ro' movements). All this allows a more rapid distribution of goods.

Forwarding freight by air

The procedure is similar to that for shipping, with these differences: the goods are usually collected by the air freight forwarder and taken into its premises prior to being delivered to the airline sheds at the airport. Many forwarders will give quotations on a door-to-door basis. The document of carriage is called an air way-bill, and is not a document of title.

The British International Freight Association★ will supply the names of registered freight forwarders, both for shipping and air freight, as well as a booklet (E2), *A Brief Introduction to Freight Forwarding*.

A particularly rapid way of sending goods by air is through the use of express air services; these are overnight carriers which deal directly with exporters, use simple documentation, and arrange for goods to be cleared through customs.

Exporting by post (international parcels)

If the goods you are exporting are neither bulky nor heavy, it may be preferable to send them by air parcel post directly to the customers. The procedure is simple: you complete the appropriate customs declaration forms (obtainable from the post office) and either attach them to the parcel or hand them in when posting. Goods sent by letter post within the European Union do not need customs declarations.

Every country has its own regulations as to customs declaration forms, packing and prohibited goods. Consult the staff at your nearest main post office when despatching each consignment. More details are available from your Royal Mail Sales Centre.★

Customs

If you are exporting within the European Union, very few forms are now required, and those that are may be mainly for statistical purposes. If you are exporting outside the European Union, contact your local Customs and Excise enquiry centre for the relevant documentation. Note that the exporter/manufacturer bears full responsibility for the declaration of the correct completion of the customs declaration, even though the forms may have been completed by someone else – the freight forwarder acting as the agent, or any other person.

Calculating your prices

In order to calculate the price to your customer abroad, you must have the following items of information:

- the amount of any discounts for cash or quantity that your supplier will allow you (unless you are exporting your own goods)

- any extra costs for export packing
- cost of freight and transportation expenses; your forwarding agent will calculate these for you
- bank charges; imposed by the bank through which you receive payment. They depend on the payment method chosen
- any costs for currency exchange
- insurance cost for CIP quotations; you must also allow for the cost of insurance for the goods in transit from the works, factory or store in this country to the docks if this is not included in the supplier's price; in some cases you may need a seller's interest policy even for an f.o.b. quote; you may need to add a credit insurance premium
- commission for your agent abroad, if you have one
- your own profit.

VAT on exports

Exports to a country outside the European Union (EU) are zero-rated for VAT, which means that you do not have to charge VAT on them, but can still reclaim the VAT on business purchases (see Chapter 7).

However, if you are exporting within the EU there are strict conditions you must meet to qualify for zero-rating. You must make sure that the goods are despatched to a destination outside the UK, and have evidence that this has happened: and you must show the customer's VAT registration number with a prefix showing the country (your own VAT number must be prefixed 'GB'). Unless your EU sales are very small, you must also send Customs and Excise a regular 'EC Sales List' of your exports to VAT-registered customers.

If you have an EU trade customer who is not VAT-registered, you may still qualify for zero-rating, but there are extra conditions to meet. However, if you are selling to private individuals in the European Union, you are technically 'distance selling' and must normally charge UK VAT – and, if your sales to one EU state rise above an annual threshold of about £70,000, you will have to register for VAT in that state.

Your local Customs and Excise office can provide the following explanatory leaflets: *Exports and Removals of Goods from the UK* (703), *VAT Retail Exports* (704), *Should I be Registered for VAT? Distance Selling* (700/1A) and *The Single Market* (725).

Insurance

You will need to find a reputable insurance company, probably through an insurance broker, to insure all your shipments. The insurer should supply you with a list of tariffs for different countries and types of risk. It will require information about each individual consignment, and will then quote accordingly.

When your responsibility for the goods ceases depends on the terms agreed with your customer. In some cases, for example if you are receiving payment through a letter of credit, you will be instructed exactly how to insure the consignment, since marine insurance forms part of the shipping documents.

Payment for exports

The four most common methods of payment for export orders are as follows (in descending order of security):

Cash with order/cash before delivery

This is the most desirable method. You may not get it – it may be prohibited under local exchange control regulations – but you can always ask.

Documentary letter of credit

With this method the exporter receives payment from a bank after presenting a complete set of documents precisely conforming to the requirements of the credit within the time limit specified in the credit.

The customer, having accepted your quotation, opens a letter of credit in your favour: that is, he or she instructs the bank abroad to instruct a bank in Britain to pay you the agreed amount, on production of a correct and complete set of documents (hence 'documentary') and on satisfying any other agreed conditions.

There are several types of letter of credit (L/C for short). The most desirable is an irrevocable letter of credit confirmed (i.e., underwritten) by a recognised bank in Britain. Payment is guaranteed in all circumstances – revolution, currency crash, insolvency, act of God included. This type of L/C is the hardest of all to come by.

There are many other forms of letter of credit, including unconfirmed irrevocable credits, and revocable letters of credit, which may facilitate payment, but are not secure. Use these when the importer is trustworthy, and his country's exchange controls require an L/C.

Forwarding documents for letters of credit

The complete set of documents required will be listed in the bank's advice of the credit, and may include one or possibly several copies of the following:

* the original letter of credit
* the exporter's commercial invoice, signed (not the pro-forma, although it contains the same information)
* the bill of lading or a receipted waybill
* the insurance policy or certificate
* bill of exchange or a sight draft (which are demands for payment)
* a certificate of origin (issued and certified by a designated UK Chamber of Commerce) specifying the origin of the goods. Details of designated Chambers in the UK may be obtained from the British Chambers of Commerce★
* export and import licences
* inspection certificates
* health certificates
* consular invoices.

Whether or not all these documents are specified in the letter of credit, many of them will be required, in any case, by the buyer, for import purposes.

All the documents must conform in every particular to the requirements of the letter of credit and to the customer's order with regard to the type and quantity of the goods, the marks (which identify the goods) and the measurements of the packing cases.

If there are any discrepancies, the bank is likely to withhold payment. And since the customer will be unable to claim the goods until the documents arrive at his or her end (forwarded by the bank), he or she may have to pay the cost of storing them in a warehouse – for which the customer will want to be reimbursed by the exporter.

Many document presentations are rejected because the documents are incorrect, or late, or both. If you are not absolutely sure of how to handle letters of credit, take advice from someone experienced in the export trade.

Payment against documentary collection

This method should be used only with a tried and proven customer: although banks are involved they act only as intermediaries and offer no guarantee of payment. The customer, in turn, must trust the exporter to supply goods of the exact type and quantity ordered: he or she undertakes to pay on a specified date (usually the arrival of the documents which prove ownership at the bank overseas or, in practice, on the arrival of the goods at the destination). The same documents as for a letter of credit are required. The bank will release the documents to the customer (thus enabling him or her to claim the goods) when it has collected the payment.

The terms of payment should be specified. You can ask for payment either on 'sight' of the documents, or, for known customers of good financial standing, you might be prepared to accept payment 30, 60 or 90 days after the customer receives the documents. If you do give credit, remember to include a reasonable allowance for interest in the price and check the credit rating of the customer. If goods are exported without an explicit arrangement to an unknown or unreliable customer, the exporter may be in a situation where there is a loss of control of the goods without any certainty of receiving payment.

Trusting to luck

You can simply send the goods and trust your customer to send you the money. If so, there are a number of international payment methods which may be used. Factors dictating which method is used are cost, security, speed and currency risk.

Increasingly, international payments are electronic, and SWIFT is the abbreviated title of the inter-bank worldwide system. International Money Transfers (or mail transfers) are arrangements whereby your customer's bank instructs a correspondent bank in the UK to pay you: express transfers are a speedier and costlier version. Bankers' drafts are effectively cash in your hands, so not very secure. Another option, if you do a considerable amount of business in one country, is to open a local bank account there.

Before quoting payment terms which do not guarantee payment, always check the credit rating of your customer, and use debt collectors if you are not paid in a reasonable time.

Bank overdraft has been the exporter's traditional method of filling the gap between shipment and payment, but now short-term export finance is available from several sources, to help exporters with payment delays and foreign exchange fluctuations. Most major banks have export finance schemes.

Protection against export risks

ECGD,★ the UK's official export credit insurer, is a government department designed to protect the exporter against some of the hazards of trading overseas. However, insurance for goods sold on short credit terms (e.g. consumables) is now available only from companies in the private sector.

ECGD cover, if available, can be tailored to meet the particular needs of customers – who now tend to be concentrated in the capital goods and project sectors. Protection is given not only for the export of goods but also for a range of services and earnings from overseas investments.

The protection generally works in one of two ways. Usually ECGD gives an unconditional guarantee of repayment to banks which provide overseas buyers with finance to purchase UK goods. On the other hand it can insure exporters directly against the main commercial and political risks of non-payment which can arise during the manufacturing and delivery stages of a contract.

ECGD's policies allow exporters to be paid in cash, either as goods are delivered or as work is completed. At the same time they enable UK companies to extend credit terms to their overseas buyers. Such terms can be the difference between an exporter winning or losing an order.

Private credit insurance has fewer restrictions on cover, plus the advantage of being able to combine export and domestic cover under the terms of one policy. There are several private insurers, including Coface LBF,★ NCM Credit Insurance★ and Trade Indemnity plc.★

Chapter 16

Bankruptcy

When you start up a new business you will naturally be optimistic about your prospects. However, because prompt action may enable you to avoid bankruptcy if you do find yourself in difficulties – and because you might find yourself with a customer going bankrupt – it is as well to know something about it from the start.

The Insolvency Service is the Government agency which administers and investigates the affairs of bankrupts and companies in compulsory liquidation under the Insolvency Act 1986. It has a number of useful leaflets, available from Insolvency Service Publications,* including *A Guide to Bankruptcy* and *A Guide for Creditors*.

Note, though, that different legislation applies in Scotland: in particular, individual voluntary arrangements (an alternative to bankruptcy) are not available.

You lay yourself open to bankruptcy proceedings if your financial position deteriorates so much that you are unable to pay your unsecured debts, or where it appears that there is no reasonable prospect that you will be able to pay a debt in the future. A creditor may, if you owe him or her at least £750 as an unsecured debt, serve on you a formal demand, requiring you:

- to pay the debt, or
- to give security for it, or
- to compound for the petition debt: in other words, to propose an arrangement with the petitioning creditor, so that the debt can be paid off under an agreed scheme of payments.

If the debt is a future debt, the demand will require you to establish to the reasonable satisfaction of the creditor that you will be able to pay the debt when it falls due.

If you do not comply with the demand, or make an application to a bankruptcy court (the High Court in London or certain specified county courts) to set aside the demand (for example on the grounds that the money is not due, or that you have a claim against the creditor that equals or exceeds your debt to him), the creditor may, after the expiration of 21 days (or even earlier in exceptional cases) file a bankruptcy petition in a bankruptcy court.

The bankruptcy petition will be endorsed with the day and time of the hearing, and must be served on you personally, but should this prove impossible, the court may give permission for a substituted service – for example, the post – to be used.

There is another way for a creditor to start bankruptcy proceedings (though a petition for bankruptcy is still required). When a debt is payable immediately, and the creditor can show the court that execution (or any other process issued in respect of the debt on a judgment or order of any court) has been returned unsatisfied in whole or in part – perhaps because there are no funds – that creditor may ask the court for a bankruptcy order.

The court has a discretion whether or not to make a bankruptcy order on the petition but will probably do so unless you:

- have paid off the debt
- can show that the debt is not due
- can show that there are sums owed to you by the creditor, which equal or exceed the debt due to him or her
- can show that you have made a proposal to compound or secure the debt, and that the creditor has unreasonably refused such proposal
- if the debt is a future debt, can satisfy the court that there is a reasonable prospect that you will be able to pay the debt when it falls due.

The court has the power to adjourn or stay the petition, and might do so to enable you to make proposals to secure or compound the debt, or to pay it off, possibly by instalments.

Avoiding bankruptcy proceedings

If you are in a situation where you cannot pay your debts in full, do not bury your head in the sand: it may be better to take steps yourself rather than allow a creditor to start bankruptcy proceedings against you. Bankruptcy will almost certainly involve the closure of your business and dismissal of your employees, whereas early voluntary action may tide you over the difficult patch. For help and advice, contact your local Business Link* or alternative body, which can put you in touch with suitably qualified people. They may suggest any of the following alternatives.

Informal arrangements

One step would be to write informally to all your creditors, asking them to agree to accept payments according to a schedule agreed with them all. This has the advantage of cheapness, but will only work if all your creditors agree, and still leaves you liable to bankruptcy proceedings if any one of them changes his or her mind.

Administration order

If your debts are less than £5,000 and there is a county court judgment for at least one of the debts, you can apply to that court for an administration order to be made. Such an order will provide for all your debts (whether or not there are court orders relating to them) to be paid by single weekly or monthly payments to the court. The court will accumulate the payments and distribute them to your creditors pro rata, from time to time. Provided that you keep up such payments, no steps can be taken to enforce the debts by other means.

If you have no prospect of paying off all your debts within a reasonable time, the court can, on your application, order that you pay only a limited percentage of your debts.

Voluntary agreement with creditors

The Insolvency Act 1986 provides for voluntary arrangements to be made with your creditors, by enabling you to apply for approval of a scheme whereby your debts are cleared by an offer to creditors made with the assistance of an insolvency practitioner.

After seeing an insolvency practitioner, you must first of all apply to the court for an interim order, stating in your application that you intend to make a proposal to creditors for a voluntary arrangement. In your application you must name a qualified insolvency practitioner who will help you to prepare the proposal for a voluntary arrangement. The local bankruptcy court will have a list of insolvency practitioners. If the court then makes an interim order, this will have the effect, during the period for which it is in force, of stopping any other proceedings, execution or other legal process from being commenced or continued against you or your property without the leave of the court.

No bankruptcy petition relating to you may be presented or proceeded with while the interim order is in force. The insolvency practitioner will then enquire into your debts and report to the court on your proposal for a voluntary arrangement, having normally first discussed the position with you fully at an interview. If the court is then satisfied, following the insolvency practitioner's report, that a meeting of your creditors should be summoned to consider his or her proposal, the court will direct that the period of the interim order be extended, and creditors will be given the opportunity to consider the proposal at a meeting. If over 75 per cent in value of the creditors present and voting at the meeting, either in person or by proxy, approve the proposal, it will be binding on all creditors who were notified of it. The named insolvency practitioner, or another chosen by creditors, will then supervise the arrangement. If such an arrangement is then made and honoured, you will avoid bankruptcy and the restrictions and publicity which go with it.

If your creditors do not approve the scheme, then the interim order will lapse and any creditors can take steps to enforce the debt or start bankruptcy proceedings.

Own bankruptcy petition

Finally, you may present your own petition in bankruptcy on payment of £250 deposit and a £25 fee to the court. Such a petition must be accompanied by a statement of your affairs, with details of all your debts and assets on a form provided by the court. Where your unsecured debts are less than £20,000 and your assets total at least £2,000, the court may not make an immediate bankruptcy order, but may appoint an insolvency practitioner to report on a possible voluntary arrangement with creditors, if it appears appropriate to the court to do so. Where a bankruptcy order is made, a certificate of summary administration may be made where on the hearing of a debtor's petition it appears to the court that the unsecured liabilities are less than £20,000 and that within the period of five years ending with the presentation of the petition, the debtor has neither been adjudged bankrupt, nor made a composition with the creditors in satisfaction of his or her debts, or a scheme of arrangement of his or her affairs.

Effect of bankruptcy order

The effect of a bankruptcy order is that all your assets (subject to very limited exceptions) are vested in your trustee in bankruptcy on his or her appointment, and until then come under the control of the Official Receiver in bankruptcy. Your assets include your home, and the trustee can seek an order for possession (if it is owned solely by you) or possession and sale (if it is owned jointly). The court must take into account, in considering whether or not to make such an order, the legal rights of your spouse and children to live in the home, but once one year has elapsed from the date of the trustee's appointment, the court assumes (save in exceptional circumstances) that the rights of the creditors outweigh all other considerations.

Unless you have been bankrupt previously or the court otherwise orders, you normally remain bankrupt for three years (two years in the case of a certificate of summary administration) and you are then discharged from the disabilities of a bankrupt.

On discharge, your assets in the bankruptcy remain vested in your trustee, who is able to sell them to pay off your debts, and they remain so vested in the trustee until all your debts are paid in full and the bankruptcy order is annulled.

Although the discharge releases you from most of your bankruptcy debts, you remain liable for certain debts, including any court orders in family proceedings, such as maintenance.

During the course of your bankruptcy you have a duty to complete a statement of affairs if this has not already been done, giving full details of your debts and assets. It will also assist the Official Receiver and your trustee in ascertaining your assets and getting them in. You may be required to attend a public examination, at which you will be questioned about the reasons for your insolvency and your dealing with assets. Your trustee may apply to the court for an order requiring you to make regular payments out of your income towards payment of your debts. You may be committing an offence if you fail to disclose your assets fully, or otherwise fail to co-operate with the trustee.

Under the Insolvency Act 1986, it is a criminal offence not to have kept proper accounting records of your business from a date two years prior to the presentation of the petition of bankruptcy, up to the date of the bankruptcy order or, having kept such books, not to have preserved them. The accounting records must be such as will show and explain the transactions of your business, and must include records of all cash received and paid; and, where the business deals in goods, there must be statements of annual stocktaking, and accounts of all goods sold and bought, showing (except for retail sales) the names of buyers and sellers. It is also an offence if, during the same period, you have materially contributed to or increased the extent of your insolvency by gambling or rash and hazardous speculation.

The principal disabilities of a bankrupt are that he or she commits an offence if he or she obtains, either alone or jointly, credit for more than £250 without disclosing the bankruptcy; or engages in business under a name other than that in which he or she was made bankrupt, without disclosing to the people with whom he or she is trading, the name in which he or she was made bankrupt.

Under the Company Directors Disqualification Act 1986 it is an offence (except with the court's permission) for a bankrupt either to act as a director or to be concerned in the promotion, formation or management of a limited company.

Addresses

ACAS Reader Ltd
PO Box 16
Earl Shilton
Leicester LE9 8ZZ
Tel: (01455) 852225
Fax: (01455) 852219

Advertising Standards Authority (ASA)
2 Torrington Place
London WC1E 7HW
Tel: 0171-580 5555
Fax: 0171-631 3051

Advisory, Conciliation and Arbitration Service (ACAS)
Brandon House
180 Borough High Street
London SE1 1LW
Tel: 0171-210 3000
Fax: 0171-210 3645

Association of British Insurers (ABI)
51 Gresham Street
London EC2V 7HQ
Tel: 0171-696 3333
Fax: 0171-696 8999
Web site: http://www.abi.org.uk

Association of Consulting Actuaries
1 Wardrobe Place
London EC4V 5AH
Tel: 0171-248 3163
Fax: 0171-236 1889
Email: acahelp@aca.org.uk

Bank of England
Issue Office, Threadneedle Street
London EC2R 8AH
Tel: 0171-601 4878
Fax: 0171-601 4771
Web site:
http://www.bankofengland.co.uk

Booksellers Association of Great Britain and Ireland
Minster House
272 Vauxhall Bridge Road
London SW1V 1BA
Tel: 0171-834 5477
Fax: 0171-834 8812
Email:
100437.226.1@compuserve.com

Brewers & Licensed Retailers Association (BLRA)
42 Portman Square
London W1H 0BB
Tel: 0171-486 4831
Fax: 0171-935 3991
Web site: http://www.bira.co.uk

British Chambers of Commerce (BCC)
4 Westwood House
Westwood Business Park
Coventry CV4 8HS
Tel: (01203) 694492
Fax: (01203) 694690
Email:
101473.3705@compuserve.com

British Export Association (BExA)
Broadway House
Tothill Street
London SW1H 9NQ
Tel: 0171-222 5419
Fax: 0171-799 2468

British Franchise Association (BFA)
Thames View
Newtown Road
Henley-on-Thames RG9 1HG
Tel: (01491) 578049
Fax: (01491) 573517
Email:
mailroom@british-franchise.org.uk

British Insurance and Investment Brokers Association
14 Bevis Marks, London EC3A 7NT
Tel: 0171-623 9043
Fax: 0171-626 9676
Email: enquiries@biiba.org.uk
Web site: http://www.biiba.org.uk

British International Freight Association (BIFA)
Redfern House
Browells Lane
Feltham TW13 7EP
Tel: 0181-844 2266
Fax: 0181-890 5546
Email: bifasec@msn.com
Web site: http://www.bifa.org

British Library Science Reference and Information Service
25 Southampton Buildings
London WC2A 1AW
Tel: 0171-412 7919
Fax: 0171-412 7495
Email: patents-information@bl.uk

British Venture Capital Association (BVCA)
Essex House, 12–13 Essex Street
London WC2R 3AA
Tel: 0171-240 3846
Fax: 0171-240 3849
Web site:
http://www.brainstorm.co.uk/bvca

BT (telemarketing guides)
(0800) 660099

BTG plc
101 Newington Causeway
London SE1 6BU
Tel: 0171-403 6666
Fax: 0171-403 7586
Web site: http://www.btgplc.com

Business Link (England)
Tel: (0345) 567765
Business Connect (Wales)
Tel: (0345) 969798
Business Shop (Scotland)
Tel: (0800) 787878

Chartered Institute of Patent Agents
Staple Inn Buildings
High Holborn
London WC1V 7PZ
Tel: 0171-405 9450
Fax: 0171-430 0471
Email: mail@cipa.org.uk
Web site:
http://www.cipa.org.uk/cipa

Chartered Institute of Taxation
12 Upper Belgrave Street
London SW1X 8BB
Tel: 0171-235 9381
Fax: 0171-235 2562
Web site: http://www.tax.org.uk

Coface LBF
15 Appold Street
London EC2A 2DL
Tel: 0171-325 9381
Fax: 0171-325 7699

Commission for Racial Equality
Elliot House, 10–12 Allington
Street, London SW1A 5EH
Tel: 0171-828 7022
Fax: 0171-630 7605
Web site: http://www.open.gov.uk/
cre/cre home.htm

Companies House (England and Wales)
Crown Way
Cardiff CF4 3UZ
Tel: (01222) 388588
Fax: (01222) 380900

Companies House (Scotland)
37 Castle Terrace
Edinburgh EH1 2EB
Tel: 0131-535 5800
Fax: 0131-535 5820

Companies Registry (Northern Ireland)
IDB House, 64 Chichester Street
Belfast BT1 4JX
Tel: (01232) 234488
Fax: (01232) 544888

Consumer Credit Trade Association
Tennyson House
159–163 Great Portland Street
London W1N 5FD
Tel: 0171-636 7564
Fax: 0171-323 0096

Croner's Reference Book for Self-Employed and Smaller Businesses
Croner House, London Road
Kingston-upon-Thames KT2 6SR
Tel: 0181-547 3333
Fax: 0181-547 2637
Web site: http://www.croner.co.uk

DDA Information line
Tel: (0345) 622633

Department of the Environment, Transport and the Regions
Eland House
Bressenden Place
London SW1E 5DU
Tel: 0171-890 3333

**Direct Marketing Association
(UK) Ltd**
Haymarket House
1 Oxendon Street
London SW1Y 4EE
Tel: 0171-321 2525
Fax: 0171-321 0191
Email: dma@dma.org.uk

DTI Consumer Affairs Division
Department of Trade and Industry
1 Victoria Street
London SW1H 0ET
Tel: 0171-215 5000
Fax: 0171-222 2629
Web site: http://www.dti.gov.uk

DTI Consumer Safety Publications
Admail 528
London SW1W 8YT
Tel: 0171-510 0151
Fax: 0171-510 0197

DTI 'country desks'
Tel: 0171-215 5000

DTI Euro Hotline
Tel: 0117-944 4888

DTI export publications
Tel: 0171-510 0171
Fax: 0171-510 0197

DTI Loan Guarantee Unit
Department of Trade and Industry
Small Firms Division
Level 2, St Mary's House
c/o Moorfoot
Sheffield S1 4PQ
Tel: 0114-259 7308
Fax: 0114-259 7316
Web site: http://www.dti.gov.uk

DTI Publications Orderline
Tel: 0171-510 0174

DTI Small Firms Publications
Admail 528
London SW1W 8YT
Tel: 0171-510 0169
Fax: 0171-510 0197

Dun and Bradstreet
Holmers Farm Way, High
Wycombe
Bucks HP12 4UL
Tel: (01494) 422000
Fax: (01494) 422332
Web site:
http://www.dunandbrad.co.uk

ECGD
2 Exchange Tower
Harbour Exchange Square
London E14 9GS
Tel: 0171-512 7000
Fax: 0171-512 7649
Web site:
http://www.open.gov.uk/ecgd/

**Employee Ownership Scotland
(EOS)**
Templeton Business Centre
Templeton Street
Bridgeton
Glasgow G40 1DA
Tel: 0141-554 3797
Fax: 0141-554 5163
Email: eos@sol.co.uk

Employers' Helpline
Tel: (0345) 143143
This government helpline gives, among other things, free telephone advice to employers about statutory sick pay, statutory maternity pay and National Insurance contributions. The service is intended to be particularly helpful to new or established small businesses without a separate wages department.

English Partnerships
16–18 Old Queen Street
London SW1H 9HP
Tel: 0171-976 7070
Fax: 0171-976 7740

Equal Opportunities Commission
Overseas House, Quay Street
Manchester M3 3HN
Tel: 0161-833 9244
Fax: 0161-835 1657

Exhibition Bulletin
Regent House
291 Kirkdale
London SE26 4RZ
Tel: 0181-778 2288
Fax: 0181-659 8495
Web site:
http://www.expobase.com

Export Market Information Centre (EMIC)
Tel: 0171-215 5444

Federation of Recruitment and Employment Services Ltd
36–38 Mortimer Street
London W1N 7RB
Tel: 0171-323 4300
Fax: 0171-255 2878
Web site: http://www.fres.co.uk

Federation of Small Businesses
32 Orchard Road
Lytham St Anne's FY8 1NY
Tel: (01253) 720911
Fax: (01253) 714651

Finance & Leasing Association
Imperial House
15–19 Kingsway
London WC2B 6UN
Tel: 0171-836 6511
Fax: 0171-420 9600

Financial Services Authority
Gavrelle House, 2–14 Bunhill Row
London EC1Y 8RA
Tel: (0845) 606 1234
Fax: 0171-382 5900
Web site: http://www.fsa.gov.uk

Grocer Marketing Directory
William Reed Ltd (publishers)
Broadfield Park
Crawley RH11 9RT
Tel: (01293) 613400
Fax: (01293) 613156
Web site:
http://www.foodanddrink.co.uk

Health and Safety Executive Info Line
Tel: (05415) 45500

Home Office Employers' Helpline
Tel: 0181-649 7878

HSE Books
PO Box 1999
Sudbury CO10 6FS
Tel: (01787) 881165
Fax: (01787) 313995
Web site:
http://www.open.gov.uk/hse/
hsehome.htm

Industrial Common Ownership Finance Ltd (ICOF)
115 Hamstead Road
Handsworth
Birmingham B20 2BT
Tel: 0121-523 6886
Fax: 0121-554 7117
Email: icof@icof.co.uk
Web site: http://www.icof.co.uk

Industrial Common Ownership Movement (ICOM)
Vassali House
20 Central Road
Leeds LS1 6DE
Tel: 0113-246 1737
Fax: 0113-224 0002
Email: icom@icom.org.uk

Industrial Society
Robert Hyde House
48 Bryanston Square
London W1H 7LN
Tel: 0171-262 2401
Fax: 0171-723 7375

Insolvency Service Publications
Measham Handling Centre
PO Box 100
Swadlincote DE12 7DR
Tel: (01530) 272515
Fax: (01530) 270879

Instant Muscle (IM) Ltd
Springside House
84 North End Road
London W14 9ES
Tel: 0171-603 2604
Fax: 0171-603 7346

Institute of Chartered Accountants in England and Wales
PO Box 433, Moorgate Place
London EC2P 2BJ
Tel: 0171-920 8100
Fax: 0171-920 0547
Web site: http://www.icaew.co.uk

Institute of Employment Consultants
3rd Floor
Steward House
16A Commercial Way
Woking GU21 1ET
Tel: (01483) 766442
Fax: (01483) 714979

Institute of Export
64 Clifton Street
London EC2A 4HB
Tel: 0171-247 9812
Fax: 0171-377 5343

Institute of Practitioners in Advertising (IPA)
44 Belgrave Square
London SW1X 8QS
Tel: 0171-245 7020
Fax: 0171-245 9904
Web site: http://www.ipa.co.uk

**Insurance Brokers Registration
Council**
63 St Mary Axe
London EC3A 8NB
Tel: 0171-621 1061
Fax: 0171-621 0840

**International Chamber of
Commerce**
ICC United Kingdom
14–15 Belgrave Square
London SW1X 8PS
Tel: 0171-823 2811
Fax: 0171-235 5447
Email:
106142.2273@compuserve.com

Lawyers for your Business
Tel: 0171-405 9075
Fax: 0171-611 6968

**LEnt A (London Enterprise
Agency) and LINC (Local
Investment Networking Company)**
4 Snow Hill
London EC1A 2BS
Tel: 0171-236 3000
Fax: 0171-329 0226
Email: 100716.3117@com
puserve.comlenta@itl.net

LiveWIRE
Tel: (0345) 573252

**Local Enterprise Development
UNIT (LEDU)**
Tel: (01232) 491031
Fax: (01232) 691432

Luncheon Vouchers Ltd
50 Vauxhall Bridge Road
London SW1V 2RS
Tel: 0171-834 6666
Fax: 0171-931 0700

Mailing Preference Service
Haymarket House
1 Oxendon Street
London SW1Y 4EE
Tel: 0171-766 4410

**National Association of Mutual
Guarantee Societies**
Scriven House, Richmond Road
Bowdon, Altrincham
Cheshire WA14 2TT
Tel: 0161-929 5130
Fax: 0161-929 5133
Email: nigel@scriven.nwnet.co.uk

National Computing Centre
Oxford House, Oxford Road
Manchester M1 7ED
Tel: 0161-228 6333
Fax: 0161-242 2400
Email: enquiries@incl.co.uk
Web site: http://www.ncc.co.uk

National Newspapers, Mail Order
Protection Scheme Ltd
16 Tooks Court
London EC4A 1LB
Tel: 0171-405 6806
Fax: 0171-404 0166

NCM Credit Insurance
3 Harbour Drive
Capital Waterside
Cardiff CF1 6TZ
Tel: (01222) 824000
Fax: (01222) 824003

Newman Books
32 Vauxhall Bridge Road, London
SW1V 2SS
Tel: 0171-973 6402
Fax: 0171-233 5057

**Office for Harmonisation in the
Internal Market (Trade Marks and
Designs)**
Tel: (00346) 513 9100
Fax: (00346) 513 9173
Email: him@lix.intercom.es

**Office for National Statistics
Information Services Division**
Press Office
Great George Street
London SW1P 3AQ
Tel: 0171-270 6363

**Office of the Data Protection
Registrar**
Wycliffe House, Water Lane,
Wilmslow SK9 5AF
Tel: (01625) 545745
Fax: (01625) 524510
Web site:
http://www.open.gov.uk/dpr/
dprhome.htm

Office of Fair Trading
15–25 Bream's Buildings
London EC4A 1PR
Tel: 0171-211 8000
Fax: 0171-211 8800
Web site:
http://www.open.gov.uk/oft/
ofthome.htm

Office of Fair Trading
Consumer Credit Licensing
Branch
Craven House, 40 Uxbridge Road
London W5 2BS
Tel: 0171-211 8608
Fax: 0171-211 8605

Office of Fair Trading Publications
OFT, PO Box 366
Hayes UB3 1XB
Tel: (0870) 6060321
Fax: (0870) 6070321
Web site:
http://www.open.gov.uk/oft/
ofthome.htm

Patent Office
Cardiff Road
Newport NP9 1RH
Tel: (0645) 500505
Web site:
http://www.patent.gov.uk

Patent Office
Search and Advisory Service
Tel: (01633) 811010
Fax: (01633) 811020
Email:
commercialsearches@patent.gov.uk

Periodical Publishers Association
Queen's House, 28 Kingsway
London WC2B 6JR
Tel: 0171-404 4166
Fax: 0171-464 4167
Web site: http://www.ppa.co.uk

The Prince's Youth Business Trust
18 Park Square East
London NW1 4LH
Tel: 0171-543 1234
Fax: 0171-543 1200
Web site:
http://www.princes-trust.org.uk

Redundancy Payments Service
Tel: *Helpline* (0500) 848489

Regional Development Division
Bay 3.B.42, 1 Victoria Street
London SW1H 0ET
Tel: 0171-215 2565
Fax: 0171-215 2562

Registry of Credit Unions and Industrial and Provident Societies
IDB House, 64 Chichester Street
Belfast BT1 4JX
Tel: (01232) 234488
Fax: (01232) 544844/544888
Web site: http://www.nics.gov.uk

Registry of Friendly Societies (England and Wales)
Victory House
30–34 Kingsway
London WC2B 6ES
Tel: 0171-663 5000
Fax: 0171-663 5060

Registry of Friendly Societies (Scotland)
58 Frederick Street
Edinburgh EH2 1NB
Tel: 0131-226 3224

Royal Mail Sales Centre
Tel: (0345) 950950
Fax: 0171-239 2092

Rural Development Commission
141 Castle Street
Salisbury SP1 3TP
Tel: (01722) 336255
Fax: (01722) 332769
Web site:
http://www.argonet.co.uk/rdc

Showman's Directory
Tel: (01483) 422184
Fax: (01483) 422184
Web site: http://www.
showmans-directory.co.uk

SITPRO (Simpler Trades Procedures Board)
Tel: 0171-215 0800 (helpdesk)

Society of Pension Consultants
St Bartholomew House
92 Fleet Street
London EC4Y 1DH
Tel: 0171-353 1688
Fax: 0171-353 9296

Systems Information Technology Group
Newcastle Technopole
Kings Manor
Newcastle-upon-Tyne NE1 6PA
Tel: 0191-227 3040
Fax: 0191-227 3055

Technical Help to Exporters
British Standards Institution
Information Centre
389 Chiswick High Road
London W4 4AL
Tel: 0181-996 7111
Fax: 0181-996 7048
Web site: http://www.bsi.org.uk

Telephone Preference Service
Haymarket House
1 Oxendon Street
London SW1Y 4EE
Tel: 0171-766 4420
Fax: 0171-976 1886
Web site: http://tps@dmae.org.uk

Thomson Directories
Customer Care Department
296 Farnborough Road
Farnborough GU14 7NU
Tel: (01252) 555555
Fax: (01252) 546664
Web site: http://www.
thomsons-directories.co.uk

3i plc
91 Waterloo Road
London SE1 8XP
Tel: 0171-928 3131
Fax: 0171-928 0058
Web site: http://www.3igroup.com

Trade Indemnity plc
1 Canada Square
Canary Wharf
London E14 5DX
Tel: 0171-739 4311
Fax: 0171-512 9186
Web site:
http://www.tradeindemnity.co.uk

Index

The Which? Guide to Computers

Wordprocessing, VAT and income tax calculations, business plans, sending faxes and electronic mail, using the Internet, producing high-quality illustrations and design, keeping sales and client records – all these tasks are much easier with the help of a small computer system. Whether you run a small business or want help with your domestic accounts, having the right computer will prove invaluable.

But buying a computer has never been harder: dealers are often ill-informed about their products, computer magazines assume a high level of technical knowledge, and consultants charge by the hour. Some people spend two or three times more than they need on a system that still may not do the job.

The Which? Guide to Computers looks at how to find hardware and software at sensible prices, how to avoid becoming a manufacturer's guinea-pig, or being left with something that is instantly obsolete, the best way to pay for a computer system, and how to be sure that what you buy will do the job you intended.

Paperback   216 × 135 mm   288 pages

Available from bookshops, and by post from
Which?, Dept TAZM, Castlemead,
Gascoyne Way, Hertford X, SG14 1LH

You can also order using your credit card
by phoning FREE on (0800) 252100
(quoting Dept TAZM)

Be Your Own Financial Adviser

Financial advice, like any other advice, can be good, bad or indifferent. But, armed with the right facts, and some basic techniques, you can be your own financial adviser. This guide shows you how to clarify your financial needs and create a financial plan to meet them, just as a personal adviser would do for you.

Be Your Own Financial Adviser profiles the different products (investments, savings, insurance, loans) available, shows you how they can fit into your financial plan, how to choose the type best suited to you and where to get current information about them. It alerts you to any areas where you could be losing out, such as having savings in uncompetitive accounts, or where you are taking unnecessary risks with investments.

The book also lists the points to check out when you're talking to providers of financial products or financial advisers and how to interpret the information you're given. Simply written and full of useful tips and warnings, the book puts you in charge.

Paperback   216 × 135 mm   352 pages

Available from bookshops, and by post from
Which?, Dept TAZM, Castlemead,
Gascoyne Way, Hertford X, SG14 1LH

You can also order using your credit card
by phoning FREE on (0800) 252100
(quoting Dept TAZM)

Which? Way to Save Tax

A new system of tax – self assessment – is now in force. For all taxpayers, but especially the nine million who are sent a tax return, it means new forms, new obligations, new time limits and new penalties. Now, more than ever, it is vital to get to grips with the British tax system and to make sure you are paying the right amount of tax.

Which? Way to Save Tax, from the *Which?* magazine money experts, makes the task a lot easier. It outlines your obligations as a taxpayer and shows you how to use the tax rules to your advantage, so that you are not among the many thousands who, each year, make overpayments totalling billions of pounds. It covers home, investments and pensions, whether you're employed, out of work or retired.

Written in straightforward, non-technical language, with checklists to help you see at a glance that you've covered all the essentials, *Which? Way to Save Tax*, published annually, provides independent, reliable, up-to-date advice that is difficult to find anywhere else.

Paperback   210 × 120 mm   352 pages

Available from bookshops, and by post from
Which?, Dept TAZM, Castlemead,
Gascoyne Way, Hertford X, SG14 1LH

You can also order using your credit card
by phoning FREE on (0800) 252100
(quoting Dept TAZM)